THE KING HAS COME

LEO R. VAN DOLSON

Pacific Press Publishing Association
Boise, Idaho
Oshawa, Ontario, Canada

Edited by Lincoln E. Steed
Designed by Tim Larson
Cover photo by Tad Janocinski, © The Image Bank
Inset photo by Betty Blue
Typeset in 10/12 Century Schoolbook

Copyright © 1989 by
Pacific Press Publishing Association
Printed in United States of America
All Rights Reserved

The author assumes full responsibility for all facts and quotations cited in this book.

Library of Congress Catalog Number: 89-61518

ISBN 0-8163-0861-6

Foreword

Imagine an ex-publican thinking that he could instruct the leaders and theologians of Israel! It must have taken a lot of God-inspired courage for Matthew to dare to write his Gospel. Though one of the most educated of Christ's disciples, Matthew was from the class despised by the Jews for selling their souls for the privilege of extortion.

However, by the time Matthew wrote the Gospel, his life and habits had completely changed. Because of his association with the Master, he undoubtedly gained some welcome respect, in Christian churches at least. But even then, outside of his own Gospel, he is mentioned only three times in the New Testament; twice in a general listing of the disciples, and once (see Acts 1:13) as being among the other disciples gathered in the upper room before Pentecost. Could it be that the other disciples were somewhat embarrassed to include a former publican in their number? Nevertheless, in spite of his embarrassing background, we are told by Ellen White that "the despised publican became one of the most devoted evangelists, in his own ministry following closely in his Master's steps" (*The Desire of Ages,* p. 275).

As a writer, Matthew paints the most complete word portrait of Christ to be found in the Gospels. Beginning with Christ's genealogy and the details surrounding His birth, Matthew describes Jesus' life down to the time of the giving of the gospel commission prior to His ascension.

Many references and quotations from the Old Testament are found in the book of Matthew. This fact, along with frequent references to the prophecies of the Messiah as having been fulfilled in Jesus, indicate that the writer's primary audience was the Jews. The three Synoptic Gospels (Matthew, Mark, and Luke) are addressed to three specific civilizations active in the Mediterranean area in the first century A.D. The Gospel of Mark is apparently addressed to the Romans, and the Gospel of Luke to the Greeks. Each of the Gospel writers shows awareness of those aspects of the life and teachings of Jesus that would appeal to his target audience.

To the Jews impatiently waiting for the promised Messiah, Matthew presented Jesus as King—the fulfillment of the Old Testament prophecies. Mark, seeking to appeal to the more energetic and active Romans, produced an abbreviated Gospel that portrays Christ as a man of energy and action. More of Christ's miracles are recorded in Mark than in any of the other gospels. On the other hand, Luke, writing to the more humanistic and philosophic Greeks, presented Jesus as the Son of Man, the Saviour of all men, the Friend of humanity. The Gospel of John is addressed apparently to the Christian community as a whole toward the end of the first century. One of John's obvious purposes in writing was to fill in the details of the life of Christ that were missing from the Synoptic accounts. His was the last of the Gospels to be written. John's account centers around the theme of Christ as the Son of God.

Addressing the Jews primarily, Matthew presents Jesus as the Son of David and the Son of Abraham. He is the Messiah, the Promised King. In the introductory genealogy, the writer establishes the royal ancestry of Jesus. His Gospel emphasizes the coming of the kingdom of the King.

At a time when many would-be messiahs were claiming to fulfill the Old Testament prophecies, Matthew took pains to show that Jesus alone met the prophetic requirements. In doing so he had to deal with a large number of fallacious assumptions regarding the nature of the promised King. The Jews looked forward to a political deliverer who would lead them to independence and world conquest.

I see in Matthew a clear example of the chiastic structure, in which the first and last elements of a literary work are parallel, as well as in-between elements paralleling each other. In recognizing this structure in Matthew's Gospel, we find the following arrangement:*

1.a. Introduction of the King, 1:1—4:17

    2.a. Introduction of the Kingdom, 4:18—10:42

    2.b. Response to the Kingdom, 11:1—16:20

1.b. Response to the King, 16:21—28:20

The first four chapters of Matthew introduce the King, giving His genealogy, telling the story of His unusual birth and childhood, portraying His anointing as the Messiah at His baptism, and outlining those events that signify His personal acceptance and the beginning of His appointed work—the announcement of the Kingdom of grace. This first section of Matthew's Gospel concludes with a pivotal statement, found in chapter 4:17, indicating a transition in the structure of the book: "From that time Jesus began to preach, and to say, Repent: for the kingdom of heaven is at hand." The key words are "From that time."

Skipping almost completely over Christ's first year of ministry that was largely centered in Judea, Matthew next moves into His Galilean ministry. In chapters 4 through 7, we discover what we will term Christ's introduction of His kingdom. This is followed in chapters 8 through 10 by a section that deals with the power that characterizes His Kingdom. A series of spectacular miracles demonstrate Christ's power over sin, storm, death, disease, and devils.

Beginning with the eighteenth verse of chapter 4, the rest of the Gospel is divided into six sections, each dealing with a period of activity followed by a teaching session. The book of Matthew is noted as having recorded more of Christ's dis-

---

*Another example of the chiastic structure used in the outline of a New Testament book is presented in *Interpreting the Book of Revelation,* by Kenneth Strand (Naples, FL.: Ann Arbor Publishers, 1976), pp. 44-51.

courses, such as the Sermon on the Mount and the Sermon by the Sea, than any of the other Gospels. The most extensive, of course, is that on the Mount of Blessing, outlined in chapters 5 through 7.

Chapters 11 through 16:20 indicate a mixed response on the part of Christ's hearers. The religious leaders, several of the cities, His own brothers, and His hometown rise up in opposition against His teaching. But there are some who gradually begin to accept Him for what He claims to be—especially His disciples. This section concludes with Peter's confession that Jesus is the Christ, the Son of God.

Following another pivotal transition statement in Matthew 16:21 that echoes the words "From that time . . . ," the Gospel writer moves into the final section of the book that shows Christ preparing His followers for His death and resurrection.

This work of preparation continues through chapters 19 to 25, but the emphasis in this section is on Christ's finally presenting Himself to the Jewish nation as its rightful King. Their rejection of the Messiah is epitomized in the temple controversy outlined in chapters 21:23 through 23:39.

Such rejection, rather than presenting Christ's kingship, would merely delay it until the spiritual kingdom was ready for Him. Then He would come the second time as King of kings (see Matthew 24:27).

The events of Christ's passion and resurrection, as outlined in chapters 26 through 28, establish His right to rule the world that has been wrested from Satan's claims by the greatest act of self-sacrifice ever seen in the universe. But more is to be accomplished before the kingdom finally can be established on earth, as is indicated by the fact that the Gospel closes with the great commission (see chapter 28:19, 20). The last phrase of the book " . . . even unto the end of the world," contains the certainty that there will be a time when the gospel commission has met its fulfillment, and the kingdom of the King will be set up on this earth restored. ☐

Contents

1.	The King Has Come	9
2.	The Presentation of the King	19
3.	A Voice With a Difference	29
4.	Mixing the Price Tags	37
5.	He Touches Us	47
6.	Pearls of Great Price	57
7.	The Bread of Life	67
8.	No Cross, No Crown	75
9.	Paying the Fare	85
10.	No Gate-Crashers in Heaven	95
11.	Seven Parables of Preparedness	103
12.	"He Humbled Himself"	113
13.	Undercomers Anonymous	121

Chapter 1
The King Has Come

An older woman stood next to the ruins of her bomb-shattered home in a little English village that had suffered a severe air raid. With tears streaming down her face, she exclaimed, "If only the king would come, we'd feel much better."

She voiced the deep heart-longing of innumerable millions in this sin-shattered world. But the good news is that the King *has* come. As a result, those who recognize His presence feel much better, in spite of the fact that they still live on this sin-scarred, bloodstained battlefield of the great controversy.

The king came nearly 2,000 years ago. Although the political leaders of His day generally ignored Him and refused to accept His claims, He changed the direction of this world's history by establishing a kingdom that soon will rule a world no longer marked by rebellion and sin.

What a glorious night that was when our King came, when the Infinite became an infant!

"Men knew it not, but the tidings fill[ed] heaven with rejoicing. With a deeper and more tender interest the holy beings from the world of light . . . [were] drawn to the earth. The whole world . . . [was] brighter for His presence. Above the hills of Bethlehem . . . [were] gathered an innumerable throng of angels" (*The Desire of Ages*, p. 47).

They were awaiting the signal to declare the glorious news that the King of the universe had come to earth. When that signal was given they flooded the hills with their glory. Those millions of angels could not restrain the wonder of it all.

10 THE KING HAS COME

Talk about extraterrestrial visitors! Never before or since have the inhabitants of this planet seen such a display of glorious supernatural light as that which flooded the hills of Bethlehem with the brightness of the angels' presence. *The Desire of Ages* describes it as "the brightest picture ever beheld by human eyes" (page 48).

What a sensation this unbelievable spectacle would have made in Athens, Rome, or Ephesus! But it didn't take place there. It took place in the remote hills a few miles south of Jerusalem, where Christ's ancestor, Ruth, had gleaned, and at the home of another ancestor, David.

"The King of glory stooped low to take humanity. Rude and forbidding were His earthly surroundings. His glory was veiled, that the majesty of His outward form might not become an object of attraction. . . . Jesus purposed that no attraction of an earthly nature should call men to His side. Only the beauty of heavenly truth must draw those who would follow Him" (*The Desire of Ages*, p. 43).

For the first time, the Creator of all beings, through His earth-born mother, now had a genealogy. And what a genealogy! Glance through it in Matthew 1:1-16. What do you find? I see the name of a prostitute, followed soon after by the name of a murderer; there's a polygamist or two; a sadistic killer of

COMPARISONS OF GENEALOGICAL LISTS		
Comparisons	**Matthew**	**Luke**
Number of names	41	76
Number from David on	28	41
Descent from David	Legal	Blood
Line of descent	Through Joseph	Through Mary

prophets; and some of the stubbornest, most rebellious kings of Judah. It's a strikingly human genealogy. As demonstrated by the chart which compares Matthew and Luke's genealogies, Matthew chose to present Jesus' legal genealogy through His foster father, Joseph. He also chose to use a numerological scheme of fourteen in each of three generations rather than developing a complete list as Luke did. Matthew wanted his readers to recognize that Jesus was both a son of Abraham and a son of David.

The King born in Bethlehem accomplished what no ruler before or after could hope to accomplish. Through Him all barriers of race and nationality have been abolished. Of course, geographers, historians, and politicians have yet to recognize this fact. But, as the poet puts it, "In Christ there is no East nor West, In Him no North or South." There is no chauvinism, no racial prejudice. In His kingdom there is one nationality—Christian. There is but one race—I'm tempted to say the human race, but that's not accurate, for through Him humanity has been touched by divinity. We humans have been raised to the throne of the universe to become joint heirs with the King of glory, if we will accept that privilege. It will not be forced upon any of us.

For this purpose, we are told in Philippians 2:7, the King humbled or emptied Himself. Heaven came down that the glory of the King of glory might fill our souls for the rest of eternity.

Our King has come! The world will never be the same again. In spite of all that is wrong with our world today, *our King has come,* and we all feel much better about it.

Unto You a Saviour Is Born

To the shepherds the angels gave the message that all sinners from the time of Adam had awaited: "For unto you is born this day in the city of David a Saviour, which is Christ the Lord" (Luke 2:11).

Previously, Mary had been told by Gabriel that she should "bring forth a son, and thou shalt call His name JESUS: for he shall save his people from their sins" (Matthew 1:21).

No name ever has had such impact on the world as that of

Jesus. We pray in His name. We sing about it. Children lisp it. We talk about its power. Too many use it carelessly or in anger. But is the name itself so important? Others bore that name between 4 B.C. and A.D. 31. Actually, in Hebrew, Jesus was called by the same name as the one who led the Israelites into Canaan, Joshua.

How appropriate! In the same way that Joshua led in the final act of Israel's deliverance from slavery, Jesus was to deliver His people from the slavery of sin.

Wise Men Still Find Him

Have you seen the bumper sticker that reads, "Wise Men Still Seek Him"? To my way of thinking, it misses the point. Shouldn't it read, "Wise Men Still *Find* Him"? Many seek, but few find.

A touching true story illustrates that Christmas still is a time of finding. "There could not have been a more discouraging moment in the lives of the young pastor and his wife. They had taken over a dilapidated old church that had certainly seen the last of its good days. Before this young couple had arrived, there had been beauty and pride in the church and its membership. But that was long before, and now it was just a shell of its former self.

"However, they loved it, and that love made the hurt more painful when a devastating storm came along and tore at the old, once-proud building. The pastor had been in the midst of an enthusiastic campaign to bring back some of the former beauty with paint, hammers, and nails—and love.

"Now, after the storm passed, he and his wife stood before the altar, weeping, for there, behind it, was a gaping wound. The buffeting wind had caused the plaster to break loose from the wall and crash to the floor, destroying what tiny remnant of beauty, if any, had been left. And there this ugly scar stood just a few days before Christmas.

"It was in this tragic and heartbreaking moment that the pastor brushed his own, and his wife's, tears aside. 'We've got the youth-benefit auction to attend, dear,' he said.

"Looking back over their shoulders as they left the battered church, they were solemn and discouraged, but in their hearts rang a promise: 'The Lord will provide!' Even then, however, little did they realize how wonderfully was that provision to be—and even on that very day—in a way many have come to look upon as close to miraculous.

"Still saddened, but hiding it beneath smiles, they did attend the auction and watched as bidders bought a variety of potential Christmas gifts from the auctioneer. When a very long gold-and-ivory tablecloth was displayed in its, perhaps, fifteen-foot length, there were very few bids. Obviously this somewhat pretty but very long, outdated cloth held no appeal to anyone—anyone, that is, except the young pastor and his wife.

"Their eyes met as if drawn by a simultaneous thought. Without hesitating, they bid the magnanimous sum of six and a half dollars. Nobody else could see even that little worth in it; so no one raised their bid. The pastor and his wife paid for it and hurried off to the church. There they nailed it over the hole in the plaster behind the altar.

"It was a sight to see. Loveliness not noticed by anyone but themselves at the auction glimmered from it. The tablecloth completely covered the damaged portion of the wall. Suddenly the feeling of Christmas filled the church with its warmth—perhaps for the first time in years.

"The second part of the 'miracle' took place during the day before Christmas, when the pastor saw an elderly woman standing at a bus stop near the church, shaking from the bitter cold. He told her that there would not be a bus coming along for almost an hour and invited her to step inside the church out of the cold.

"Gratefully the little woman walked toward the church with him, explaining in broken English that she was from out of town and that she was here only to answer a newspaper ad for a governess. But because of her poor English, she was not hired.

"Once inside the church, the woman gazed, wide-eyed, at the cloth hanging behind the altar. 'Lovely, isn't it?' the pastor said, pleased at the brightness in her expression.

"Then she walked quickly to the altar, palms pressed together. Full of excitement, the woman took a corner of the cloth between her fingers. The pastor smiled and went to her, but before he could speak, the woman turned her tear-filled eyes toward him.

" 'This is my banquet cloth!' she exclaimed. 'My late husband had it made specially for me in Bohemia. This is it!'

"She then related the painful story about how she and her husband had lived in Vienna until the Nazis came to power. He had seen to it that she got to the safety of Switzerland, promising that he would follow as soon as possible. As the years passed, however, she never saw him again and was eventually told that he had died in a concentration camp.

"Now, many years later, on Christmas Eve, in this country far from Vienna and Switzerland, and where the lady had been turned down for a position because her English was poor, the past was brought suddenly, startlingly, into the present. And the memories flowed with her tears.

"**The Final Chapter.** That night, as Christmas Eve services ended, an old man, who was the town clockmaker and repairman, approached the pastor. 'That cloth,' he told him, 'years ago my wife—God rest her—and I owned one exactly like it in our home in Vienna.'

"The pastor's throat tightened. He called his wife, and, together with the old man, they searched out and located the people who had advertised for a governess. From them they got the address of the woman who had applied for and been refused the job because of her poor English. Then they sought and found her.

"When the woman and the man who had thought the other dead for so many years tearfully embraced, the pastor and his wife did also. All the discouragement, disappointment, and sorrow that the cruel storm had blown into their lives now could be seen as a blessing. The Lord had truly provided—in one of His own mysterious ways" (Tom Dowling, "The Gold Tablecloth," *These Times*, December, 1978, p. 17. Copyright © 1978 by Tom Dowling).

One reason I think this Christmas story so meaningful is

that Christmas should be a time of finding—a time when, once again, we discover the Christ that Christmas is all about.

The strangest part of the entire story of the wise men from the East finding Jesus in Bethlehem, as far as I'm concerned, is that those considered to be the *wisest* people in Jerusalem at that time did not bother to seek Him; thus, they did not find Him. They knew exactly where He was to be born. They told the wise men from the East where to find Him. But they were not interested enough to take a look for themselves. Why? They were so wise in their own conceit that they ended up being ridiculed for all time as the most foolish men of their day.

Incidentally, notice that it was the star that led the wise men to Jerusalem. But it was the Scriptures that led them to Bethlehem.

We live in a time when many of the "wisest" men of our world still scoff at the story of Bethlehem. But the truly wise will find Him and worship Him—recognizing Him as the King who came down to us so that we might spend all eternity in His kingdom of glory.

Another strange thing in the story of the wise men is how little we know about them.

- *Where did they come from?* We have only a vague idea—somewhere to the east of the Holy Land.

- *How many were there?* We do not know. Tradition says three, based on the gifts that are enumerated. But there *must* have been more. It would not have been safe for three men carrying so much wealth to travel through robber-infested territory. Neither would the coming of three men have made such an impact on Jerusalem.

- *How long did it take them to get to Bethlehem?* That depends on where they came from. They saw the star the night the angels appeared to the shepherds. "As the light faded, a luminous star appeared, and lingered in the sky. It was not a fixed star nor a planet, and the phenomenon excited the keenest interest. That star was a distant company of shining angels, but of this the wise men were ignorant" (*The Desire of Ages*, p. 60).

When they arrived in Bethlehem, Jesus and His parents were living in a house, not still in the stable, according to Matthew 2:11. That verse also speaks of Him as a "child," not an infant. It must have taken the wise men at least several months to make their journey.

So, when at Christmas we sing "We Three Kings of Orient Are," remember that there probably were more than three, that they were philosophers and counselors (*magi*) rather than kings, and that they were not from what we today call the Orient!

He Came to Bring Us Gifts

The actions the wise men took when they came to Jesus are the same all must take who find Him as their Saviour today.

1. *They came*—from a long distance, as many of us do.

2. *They sought*—Where did they seek? In Jerusalem; that's where they would have expected to find a king. But He wasn't there. We do not always find Him where we expect to today either.

3. *They found*—Not in a palace, but in a humble home in an unpretentious mountain village.

4. *They worshiped*—They did not come out of idle curiosity. They came to adore and worship the greatest King of all time.

Notice that an important part of their worship was to bring Him gifts. That would be expected. But what important part did their gifts play. We have this insight: "Satan was bent on shutting out the divine light from the world, and he used his utmost cunning to destroy the Saviour. But He who never slumbers or sleeps was watching over His beloved Son. He . . . provided in a heathen land a refuge for Mary and the child Jesus. And through the gifts of the magi from a heathen country, the Lord supplied the means for the journey into Egypt and the sojourn in a land of strangers" (*The Desire of Ages*, p. 65).

But do you realize that their gifts were but a token of the greatest gift of all that God gave us that first Christmas through His Son? Today when we come to Jesus, He provides the gold, incense, and myrrh that we need in order to come *out* of the Egypt of sin. In the Laodicean message of Revelation 3 the gifts are listed in the same order that they are mentioned in Matthew 2:

1. *Gold.* The purest gold that has been "tried in the fire" (Revelation 3:18). Ellen White often referred to it as "faith that works by love and purifies the soul." (See *Faith and Works*, pp. 48, 49 and Selected Messages, vol. 1, pp. 349, 374, 398.)

2. *Frankincense.* It was used in the temple in Jerusalem as one of the ingredients of the sacred incense burned on the altar in the first apartment. That sacred service is linked closely with Jesus' intercessory ministry that makes it possible for our sins to be forgiven and for us to be clothed with His pure garment of righteousness. That same figure is used in the second prescription Jesus gives to enable us to overcome our Laodicean sleeping sickness in Revelation 3:18. He counsels us to come to Him for "white raiment, that thou mayest be clothed, and that the shame of thy nakedness do not appear."

3. *Myrrh.* This was an ingredient used in compounding the holy anointing oil used in connection with the sanctuary service (see Exodus 30:22-30). As such, it can be linked readily with the eyesalve Jesus provides to cure the spiritual blindness of His Laodicean people. In each case, the oil or the eyesalve represents the Holy Spirit, who alone can lead us to recognize our need and turn to our Lord who will provide all we need.

In a sense, then, it is Jesus who brings us the gold, frankincense, and myrrh as His Christmas gifts to us today. There is no greater gift. Through these symbols He provides our salvation. Although they are listed in the order of their value in the Laodicean message, we must receive them in the order that follows:

First, the anointing oil or eyesalve of the Spirit in order to recognize our need.

Second, the frankincense of His forgiving ministry that covers us with the glorious pure robe of His perfect righteousness.

Third, the gold of a true faith that works by love and purifies our souls.

Of course, we cannot force Christmas gifts on our friends and relatives. They are not truly gifts unless voluntarily accepted and appreciated. And Jesus does not force His Christmas gifts on us today. But He urges us to receive them by receiving Him: "Behold," He pleads, "I stand at the door, and knock: if any man hear my voice, and open the door, I will come in to him, and will sup with him, and he with me. To him that overcometh will I grant to sit with me in my throne, even as I also overcame, and am set down with my Father in his throne. He that hath an ear, let him hear what the Spirit saith unto the churches" (Revelation 3:20-22).

Chapter 2
The Presentation of the King

According to the prophet Isaiah, before the "glory of the Lord shall be revealed" (Isaiah 40:5) in the life and ministry of Jesus, one would come who would be a "voice . . . that crieth in the wilderness, Prepare ye the way of the Lord" (Isaiah 40:3).

The last Old Testament prophet, Malachi, predicted, "Behold, I will send you Elijah the prophet before the coming of the great and dreadful day of the Lord" (Malachi 4:5).

Both prophecies were fulfilled initially through John the Baptist. John proclaimed himself to be Isaiah's "voice of one crying in the wilderness" (John 1:23), and Jesus tied the Elijah symbol to the Baptist (see Matthew 11:14).

However, the ultimate and greatest fulfillment of these prophecies is to take place in the life and ministry of those who prepare the way for Jesus' second coming. Those whose lives demonstrate the full outworking of Christ in the heart are modern-day Elijahs and John the Baptists. They will be used by God to finish His work and prepare for the second coming of Christ in the midst of a world that has abandoned biblical morality and is characterized by a severe generation gap. Concerning this generation gap, the prophet we call Malachi predicted that the people of God who come in the spirit and power of Elijah will "turn the heart of the fathers to the children, and the heart of the children to their fathers" (Malachi 4:6). A careful study of how John the Baptist prepared God's people for Christ's first coming is instructive to those called to be voices crying in the spiritual wilderness of these last days.

"Our message must be as direct as was that of John. He rebuked kings for their iniquity. Notwithstanding the peril his life was in, he never allowed truth to languish on his lips. Our work in this age must be as faithfully done. . . .

"In this time of well-nigh universal apostasy, God calls upon His messengers to proclaim His law in the spirit and power of Elias. As John the Baptist, in preparing a people for Christ's first advent, called their attention to the Ten Commandments, so we are to give, with no uncertain sound, the message: 'Fear God, and give glory to him; for the hour of his judgment is come.' With the earnestness that characterized Elijah the prophet and John the Baptist, we are to strive to prepare the way for Christ's second advent" (Ellen G. White Comments, *SDA Bible Commentary*, vol. 4, p. 1184).

John's Ministry

Judah had not had a prophet for four centuries. Then, suddenly, an old-fashioned, sin-denouncing, tell-it-like-it-is, honest-to-goodness prophet appeared. What a sensation! Even in the terrible summer heat, the crowds flocked to the Jordan valley to listen as the voice of prophecy called the nation to an awareness of backsliding and the need of reform. Most of those who came out of curiosity did not even sense their need. They thought they were on the royal road to heaven because of who they were. Both John and Jesus had to use the "shock treatment" in their ministry to startle these self-satisfied people from their lethargy.

Because so many believed that salvation was assured to those who could trace their lineage back to Abraham, John, preaching in the rocky desert, told them, "Out of these stones God can raise up children for Abraham" (Matthew 3:9, NIV). He challenged them to give evidence in their lives that they were sons and daughters of God.

John's special mission was to bring the people to a sense of their need for the ministry of the Messiah who was to follow. "Before the seed of the gospel could find lodgment, the soil of the heart must be broken up. Before they would seek healing from Jesus, they must be awakened to their danger from the wounds of sin" (*The Desire of Ages*, p. 104).

Added to John's shocking message was his startling adaptation of the Jewish practice of proselyte baptism. Up until that time baptism had been used mostly as a ceremony for inducting proselytes into the Jewish religion. John turned it into a rite through which people acknowledged their need for repentance and testified to their decision to begin a new way of life by God's grace. Without such a commitment they would not be ready for a place in Christ's kingdom.

The Baptism

People of all classes flocked to the wilderness to hear the startling message of the first prophet sent in four hundred years to call the nation to repentance. One of those who came was John, the son of Zebedee, a prosperous fisherman who lived on the shores of Lake Galilee. He journeyed to the place along the Jordan where John was preaching. His young, tender heart responded to the thrilling announcement that the Messiah soon would come. Gladly this John repented, was baptized, and stayed by to become a disciple of the other John (see John 1:35).

As the time arrived for Jesus to become known publicly, John the Baptist proclaimed that One was coming after him who was greater than he (see Matthew 3:11). When Jesus presented Himself for baptism, the Baptist had been preaching about the coming Messiah for less than a year. Apparently the son of Zebedee was present to hear the exchange when the Baptist protested to Jesus that he was not worthy to baptize the Messiah. How could, and why should, he, a sinner, baptize the pure, sinless Son of God?

Jesus explained that He was setting an example for His followers. "Jesus did not receive baptism as a confession of guilt on His own account. He identified Himself with sinners, taking the steps that we are to take, and doing the work that we must do. His life of suffering and patient endurance after His baptism was also an example to us" (*The Desire of Ages*, p. 111).

What did Jesus mean when he explained to John the Baptist that "it becometh us to fulfil all righteousness?" "He came to fulfill all righteousness, and, as the head of humanity, to show man that he can do the same work, meeting every specification of the requirements of God. Through the measure of His grace furnished to the human agent, not one need miss heaven. Perfection of character is attainable by every one who strives for it. This is made the very foundation of the new covenant of the gospel" (*Selected Messages*, bk. 1, pp. 211, 212).

Jesus' baptism marked the beginning of His mission. Jesus rose from the water to begin His ministry of inviting men and women to become citizens of the kingdom of God. Just so, our baptism marks the beginning of our mission for Him. At baptism, Christians dedicate themselves to the Lord's service.

From the Dove to the Devil

After the Spirit of God descended on Jesus at His baptism and He heard the comforting words, "This is my beloved Son," the Spirit led Him into the wilderness to meet the devil's insidious challenge of "*If* thou be the Son of God." Satan attempted to do everything possible to cause Jesus to doubt that He had correctly understood the voice at the Jordan.

"When Jesus was led into the wilderness to be tempted, He was led by the Spirit of God. He did not invite temptation. He went to the wilderness to be alone, to contemplate His mission and work. By fasting and prayer He was to brace Himself for the bloodstained path He must travel. But Satan knew that the Saviour had gone into the wilderness, and he thought this the best time to approach Him" (*The Desire of Ages*, p. 114).

John the son of Zebedee had heard the voice proclaim Jesus the Son of God. After a time, he followed Jesus to the place where he was tempted. "John, one of the new disciples, had searched for Christ and had found Him in His humiliation, emaciated, and bearing the marks of great physical and mental distress. Jesus, unwilling that John should witness His humiliation, had gently yet firmly dismissed him from His presence. He wished to be alone; no human eye must behold

THE PRESENTATION OF THE KING 23

His agony, no human heart be called out in sympathy with His distress" (Ellen G. White Comments, *SDA Bible Commentary*, vol. 5, p. 1132).

We should never place ourselves in a position where we know we will be tempted. Jesus did not go into the wilderness to invite temptation, but to be alone, to contemplate His approach to ministry, and, by fasting and prayer, to prepare Himself for the difficult years of ministry ahead. The thought of the struggle with the powers of darkness that He faced made Him insensible to His physical needs. His soul was fed on the bread of life. After Jesus had fasted for nearly six weeks, Satan appeared to Him as an angel of light in order to tempt Him. The devil always seeks to take advantage of us in our weakest moments. Physically, this was the lowest point in Christ's life. But I believe that the devil miscalculated; for, spiritually, the Lord was well prepared to meet temptation.

Hebrews 4:15 tells us that Christ was tempted in the same points that we are. Some claim that Jesus never had a chance to be tempted by such temptations we have today. Such temptations as cigarettes, pool halls, and television. It is true that Jesus did not meet every possible temptation we face, but His human nature was tempted on every basic point that we have to face. Temptation can be summarized in three categories:

1. **The physical.** He was tested first on **appetite,** the "lusts of the flesh." Satan seeks to gain access to us through the senses and the physical being. This is one of His most successful means of leading us into sin. As he learned through tempting Adam and Eve, we humans can be tempted rather easily to doubt God's care and ability to provide for all our needs.

2. **The mental.** Jesus' second test was on **avarice,** the "lust of the eyes," the visualization of sin, the desire to do and get that which God has not seen fit as yet to provide. The subtlety of the devil's suggestion is revealed by James Stalker in his *Life of Jesus Christ*: "The suggestion that He should leap from the pinnacle of the temple was probably also a tempta-

tion to gratify the vulgar desire for wonders, because it was a part of the popular belief that the Messiah should appear suddenly, and in some marvelous way; as, for instance, by a leap from the temple roof into the midst of the crowds assembled below" (Westwood, N.J.: Fleming H. Revell Co., 1949, pp. 43, 44). Had Jesus responded by such a display, He would have taken a step outside the divine will. We call that *presumption.* Satan still tempts us to presumption today, to take into our own hands what we think needs to be accomplished rather than waiting for God to lead the way.

3. **The Spiritual.** Jesus next was tested on **ambition,** the "pride of life," on putting the love of the world and its honor above love and service to God. Satan offered Christ what appeared to be an easy way out. Why should He go through all the trouble, trial, and torture that lay ahead? It would be much simpler just to acknowledge that in his present human form, Satan was superior to Him. Then Satan would give Him the rulership of the world that He seemed to want so much. This suggestion subtly ignored the fact that only God should be worshiped and that Christ still was divine, even though He had taken forever our human nature. The challenge such a temptation presents to us today is to keep our priorities straight and to seek first the kingdom of God.

Christ's victory over Satan was just as complete as had been Adam's failure in the Garden of Eden. We cannot excuse ourselves for failure by pointing to our inheritance from Adam. We can overcome as Jesus overcame. "There was in Him nothing that responded to Satan's sophistry. He did not consent to sin. Not even by a thought did He yield to temptation. *So it may be with us.* Christ's humanity was united with divinity; He was fitted for the conflict by the indwelling of the Holy Spirit. And He came to make us partakers of the divine nature. So long as we are united to Him by faith, sin has no more dominion over us. God reaches for the hand of faith in us to direct it to lay fast hold upon the divinity of Christ, that we may attain to perfection of character.

And how this is accomplished, Christ has shown us. By what means did He overcome in the conflict with Satan? By

THE PRESENTATION OF THE KING

the Word of God" (*The Desire of Ages*, p. 123, italics supplied).

"Behold the Lamb"

John the Baptist "was acquainted with the events that had marked the birth of Jesus. He had heard of [Jesus'] visit to Jerusalem in His boyhood, and of what had passed in the school of the rabbis. He knew of His sinless life, and believed Him to be the Messiah; but of this he had no positive assurance. The fact that Jesus had for so many years remained in obscurity, giving no special evidence of His mission, gave occasion for doubt as to whether He could be the Promised One. The Baptist, however, waited in faith, believing that in God's own time all would be made plain. It had been revealed to him that the Messiah would seek baptism at his hands, and that a sign of His divine character should then be given. Thus he would be enabled to present Him to the people" (*The Desire of Ages*, pp. 109, 110).

When John heard the voice from heaven he knew that Jesus was the Messiah. "The Holy Spirit rested upon him, and with outstretched hand pointing to Jesus, he cried, 'Behold the Lamb of God, which taketh away the sin of the world'" (*The Desire of Ages*, p. 112).

John himself was startled by the words the Holy Spirit put in his mouth. Because he was not sure of their import, he studied the prophecies and the sacrificial system intently during the weeks that followed, and began to understand more clearly that Jesus had come to be a suffering sacrifice as well as a conquering king.

Toward the end of the century, the apostle John wrote his eyewitness account of what happened after the temptation. Matthew does not record this detail, but it is necessary for us to review the apostles' account in order to complete the picture.

John the Baptist had moved to the area of Bethabara beyond Jordan to continue his preaching and baptizing. Many of those who had been present when Jesus was baptized followed the Baptist to this new location, including the other John, the future apostle.

The Baptist, suddenly aware that Jesus was standing there in the crowd, announced, "Among you stands one you do not know. He is the one who comes after me, the thongs of whose sandals I am not worthy to untie" (John 1:26, 27, NIV). But Jesus made no move to identify Himself.

"The next day John seeth Jesus coming unto him, and saith, Behold the Lamb of God, which taketh away the sin of the world." "I saw the Spirit descending from heaven like a dove, and it abode upon him." "And I . . . bare record that this is the Son of God" (John 1:29, 32, 34).

Many of the people who looked at Jesus, emaciated after His ordeal in the wilderness and dressed in a simple Galilean homespun garment, found it difficult to accept John's testimony. However, some were impressed by the atmosphere of power and love that surrounded Him.

"On the following day, while two disciples were standing near, John [the Baptist] again saw Jesus among the people. Again the face of the prophet was lighted up with glory from the Unseen, as he cried, 'Behold the Lamb of God!' The words thrilled the hearts of the disciples. . . .

"Leaving John, they went to seek Jesus. One of the two was Andrew, the brother of Simon; the other was John the evangelist. These were Christ's first disciples" (*The Desire of Ages*, p. 138).

"Follow Me"

Matthew does not record the following year of Christ's ministry in Judea. We have to depend on John's eyewitness account for what little we know of that period of the Saviour's life. The Gospel accounts do tell us that Andrew called His brother, Simon Peter, to join him in following Jesus, and that after Jesus called Philip to follow Him, Philip led Nathaniel to become a follower of the Master. But it was not until a year later that, according to Matthew's account, Jesus established His headquarters in Peter's hometown of Capernaum.

Why Capernaum? One reason was that He had been rejected by Nazareth, His own hometown in Galilee. Also, it was a border town, as can be seen by the fact that there was a custom house there, surrounded by Gentile nations. It also was on one of the main routes of travel. Thus it was fairly large and more cosmopolitan than most Galilean communities, providing an audience that would be more acceptant to some of Jesus' rather revolutionary teachings.

Up until the time Jesus moved to Capernaum, none of His followers had joined Him as full-time laborers in His cause. But after Peter and Andrew had spent a night fishing without success, Jesus appeared to them as they approached the shore. He requisitioned Peter's boat to deliver His "sermon by the sea" to the multitude that had gathered quickly to hear Him. Then He turned to Peter and told him to go out fishing again. Because night was the best time for net fishing and they had caught nothing the previous night, Peter did not see any use in fishing any more that day. But, in his love for Jesus, he did what the Master suggested. As Simon and Andrew lowered their net, they were amazed to see it fill quickly with fish. When they got to shore, they had to enlist James and John to help them secure the great load. At that point, Jesus called them to special full-time service, inviting, "Follow me, and I will make you fishers of men" (Matthew 4:19). It must have been a temptation to them to wait until they could reap and enjoy the profits from the great catch of fish, but Matthew records, "At once they left their nets and followed him" (Matthew 4:20, NIV).

Matthew seems greatly impressed with their immediate response. After Jesus called the four fishermen to discipleship, Matthew was the next to be called. When he was seated at his custom booth one day, Jesus stood before the publican, bidding him, "Follow me." "And he left all, rose up, and followed him" (Luke 5:28). "There was no hesitation, no questioning, no thought of the lucrative business to be exchanged for poverty and hardship. It was enough for him that he was to be with Jesus. . . .

"To Matthew in his wealth, and to Andrew and Peter in their poverty, the same test was brought; the same consecration was made by each. At the moment of success, when the nets were filled with fish, and the impulses of the old life were strongest, Jesus asked the disciples at the sea to leave all for the work of the gospel. So every soul is tested as to whether the desire for temporal good or for fellowship with Christ is strongest" (*The Desire of Ages*, p. 273).

Matthew beheld the Lamb. It didn't take him long to decide that he wanted to follow Jesus and be changed into His image. In the same way, we need to fix our eyes upon "the Lamb of God, which taketh away the sin of the world." By beholding we will be changed to be like Jesus. "Looking unto Jesus, we shall be ashamed of our coldness, our lethargy, our self-seeking. We shall be willing to be anything or nothing, so that we may do heart service for the Master" (*The Desire of Ages*, pp. 439, 440).

How much does Jesus love us? Have you seen the plaque that so dramatically expresses God's love? It reads:

"I asked Jesus, 'How much do you love me?'

"And Jesus said, 'This much,'

and He stretched out His arms and died for me."

> "O that the world might taste and see
> The riches of His grace!
> The arms of love that compass me
> Would all mankind embrace.
> "His only righteousness I show,
> His saving truth proclaim.
> 'Tis all my business here below
> To cry, Behold the Lamb!"
> —Wesley

Chapter 3
A Voice With a Difference

Many voices beckon to us with the siren song "Come here and see what we have to offer." Everything from soap ads to blurbs for pleasure cruises promise us much but deliver precious little. I suppose it always has been that way since the first distorted claim made by the serpent in the Garden of Eden. It seems that everyone has a different prescription for happiness.

That is also the way it was when Jesus delivered His Sermon on the Mount. There were many teachers in His time who stated, "Many paths lead to the reality of truth and life." Even then, Rabbi Wise, Doctor of Philosophy, and Guru Mystic hypothesized that there is truth in each approach to life. "Take your choice," they suggested. "There's more than one way to look at things." And the more people listened to that nonsense, the more confused they became. It was difficult to know what to believe.

Then they heard the voice from the mount of Beatitudes—a voice with a difference. It was authoritative and convincing. Yet it phrased ideas in simple language that everyone could understand. Because truth carries its own verification, the people who listened that day to the voice of Jesus, and the multitudes who have listened ever since, recognized the simplicity and beauty of eternal truth.

The Sermon on the Mount was Jesus' ordination address to His disciples. As He began to speak to them, others began to flock around Him to hear what He had to say. Because the narrow beach on which He was standing "did not afford even standing room within reach of His voice for all who desired to hear Him, . . . Jesus led the way back to the mountainside. Reaching a level space that offered a pleasant gathering place for the vast assembly, He seated Himself on the grass, and the disciples and the multitude followed His example" (*The Desire of Ages*, p. 298).

On the mountainside, in words that all could understand and treasure, Jesus outlined seven simple steps for those who want to become God's sons and daughters—citizens of His eternal kingdom. The first several verses of Matthew 5 contain Christ's answer to such pressing problems of life as pride, insecurity, sin, guilt, despair, and disillusionment. The Beatitudes offer a line of progression to the kind of happiness and peace that come from the realization that we belong to God.

"Christ proclaims that the main objective of the kingdom is to restore the lost happiness of Eden to the hearts of men, and that those who choose to enter in by the 'strait' gate and the 'narrow' way (Matthew 7:13, 14) will find true happiness. They will find inward peace and joy, true and lasting satisfaction for heart and soul that come only when 'the peace of God that passeth all understanding,' is present to keep their 'hearts and minds through Christ Jesus' (Phillipians 4:7)" (*SDA Bible Commentary*, vol. 5, p. 324).

Seven Steps

Christ's seven steps to becoming children of God include the following practical measures that we take when His grace is at work in our lives:

1. Recognizing our need and being willing to let Him do something about it.
2. Being sorry for and turning from sin.
3. Submitting ourselves fully to God's will for us.
4. Being filled with the water of life and the bread of life (justification and sanctification).
5. Sharing what we have experienced with those about us.

6. Partaking of His purity and integrity.
7. Enjoying the peace that passes understanding and demonstrating our contentment to all about us.

When we can be recognized as "peacemakers" we "shall be called the children of God" (Matthew 5:9). To be peacemakers we must have Christ's peace and contentment in our lives. When we have it, we will not hoard it. The seventh beatitude does not place God's blessing on those who *have* peace, but on those who *share* it.

A strangely contradictory statement seems to follow in Matthew 5. Somehow we have the idea that peace is the absence of strife, hardship, and trouble. But that reflects only a shallow concept of peace—the peace-at-any-price philosophy. Jesus pointed out that the peace the children of God have comes from a strong confidence and sense of security in their loving God. They know He will care for and provide for them, no matter what happens. So Jesus added to the seven steps a blessing that would reassure those who become children of God. They should know that the hand of a loving Father still keeps them in spite of the inevitable earthly misunderstandings that result when they begin living for Christ.

When our lives begin to reflect the character of Christ, we can expect to be confronted with the same kind of opposition that He met. In fact, when there is no opposition to our witness, we might do well to question whether we are living as children of God should be living.

Jesus does not present us with the hope of enjoying a life free from trial. Instead He offers us the privilege of walking with Him in the pathway of self-denial and reproach. But He does promise us the strength to bear His cross and share His humiliation before we, at last, share in His eternal glory.

Just before His death, Jesus reminded the disciples that they would suffer many things because of their witness for Him (see John 15:20, 21). There's a hidden purpose in it all. "Through trials and persecution, the glory—character—of God is revealed in His chosen ones. The church of God, hated and persecuted by the world, are educated and disciplined in the school of Christ. They walk in narrow paths on earth; they are purified in the furnace of affliction. They follow Christ through sore conflicts; they endure self-denial and experience bitter disappointments; but their painful experience teaches them the guilt and woe of sin, and they look upon it with abhorrence. Being partakers of Christ's sufferings, they are destined to be partakers of His glory" (*Thoughts From the Mount of Blessing*, p. 31).

Sharing Christ's Righteousness

As a result of our closeness to Christ and that which He does in leading us to become children of God, He tells us that we will be "the salt of the earth" and "the light of the world" (Matthew 5:13, 14).

As the light of the world, Jesus said, "A city that is set on a hill cannot be hid" (Matthew 5:14). That was true long before the world knew anything about electric lights and neon signs. For defensive purposes many of the cities of ancient Palestine were built on hilltops. So the people Jesus spoke to understood what He meant when He pointed out that their light could be seen from great distances.

What will they see? Jesus answers, "Let your light so shine before men, that they may see your good works, and glorify your Father which is in heaven" (verse 16).

But it really is *not* our good works they see, nor is it *our* light. What they see is Jesus in us. The beauty and sunshine of His love and character so fill our souls that they overflow to those about us. The prophet Isaiah saw that this would be the result even in the darkest period of earth's history, just before the dawn of eternal day. Through him God challenges us, "Arise, shine; for thy light is come, and the glory of the Lord is risen upon thee. For, behold, the darkness shall cover the earth, and gross darkness the people: but the Lord shall arise upon thee, and *his* glory shall be seen upon thee" (Isaiah 60:1, 2, italics supplied).

And what is to be the response of the world that is wrapped in gloom and despair? "And the Gentiles shall come to thy light, and kings to the brightness of thy rising" (verse 3). It has to begin somewhere, sometime, and with someone. It can begin here and now, with you and me, if we will let His glorious light fill our hearts and souls so that the glory of the Lord may be seen in us.

What Everybody Ought to "No"

There is not a word in the Beatitudes about being blessed or happy by strict pharisaical obedience to the commandments. The Pharisees who were listening critically to everything Jesus was saying could not help but observe this fact. They were about to accuse Him of doing away with the law of God when Jesus, reading their hearts, brought up the issue before they could. "Think not," He said, reading their hearts, "that I am come to destroy the law, or the prophets" (Matthew 5:17). He went on to explain that He was doing just the opposite, putting them back in their proper sphere after centuries of distortion and misunderstanding on the part of the Jewish religious teachers.

The words He spoke were so simple: "I say unto you, That except your righteousness shall exceed the righteousness of the scribes and Pharisees, ye shall in no case enter into the kingdom of heaven" (Matthew 5:20). These words brought the monumental building blocks of their philosophical castle tumbling about the ears of those pridefully pious people. Since those words were spoken, no one ever has taken the Pharisees quite as seriously. They stood clearly, exposed in all their pious pretensions, as *not being good enough.*

All they could do was mumble, "That's ridiculous. No one can be expected to live the way He says we should live." Yet they dimly realized that standing before them was One who *did* live that way. For months their spies had trailed Him, reporting His every word and act. They knew how *He* lived.

They were right in one sense. None of them and none of us can live that way unless we are transformed by a miracle of grace. Surprisingly, Christ's way is the strictest and most difficult to follow. That is, it is impossible if we try to do it on our own. That is what the problem was with the Pharisees. They were trying to do the impossible. Live up to God's laws on their own.

Clearly and convincingly Jesus illustrated how vain were the Pharisees' strivings for man-made righteousness. His loving rebuke incisively spotlighted the shallowness of their false assumptions. Six times the Man from Nazareth drove the point home. "You say, Do not kill. But God's law goes much further. It really tells you not to get angry, not to call people names. It commands you to live at peace with all men. Again, you say, Do not commit adultery. But the law actually instructs you not to lust, even by a thought. You also say, When a man puts away his wife, he must give her a notice of divorce. That's not good enough. You are not to divorce at all, except on grounds of marital infidelity. You insist, Do not break an oath sworn in the sight of God. But God does not want you to swear at all. You live by the principle, An eye for an eye, and a tooth for a tooth. But God's standard of righteousness goes far beyond that. He says that you are not to resist if someone wants to harm you. If someone wants to sue you for the shirt off your back, don't go to court; give him your overcoat too. You say, Love your friends and hate your enemies. My code of life is that you love your enemies and pray for those who persecute you. You see, only when you live the way I have outlined are you really sons and daughters of your heavenly Father" (Matthew 5:21-48, paraphrased).

Actually, the Ten Commandments are merely God's minimums of Christlike behavior. As Jesus pointed out, there are no maximums. The more Christlike we become, the greater the challenge that looms ahead. There is always room for becoming more Christlike. But it is impossible for us to accomplish it on our own. Only by God's power at work in us can we achieve those ideals that are higher than the highest human thought can reach. That is what Jesus was trying to impress on the minds of those who felt that the highest ideal was to be like the Pharisees.

Satan wants to keep us from understanding the purpose of the law and from recognizing its thrilling promise. In fact, he has tried from the inception of sin to convince the entire universe that created beings cannot live according to God's law.

But Christ came to prove just the opposite. He demonstrated, not only in His teaching, but also in His life and death, what it means to fulfill the law, to live according to its basic principles. He came to bring us a new perspective of the purpose, power, and promise of God's law.

God's laws, when properly understood, can be seen as evidence of His great love and concern for us. He is interested in every phase of our being—in the way we eat, sleep, dress, and play, as well as in the way we worship. He wants us to get the most out of life now, as well as to enjoy the blessings of immortality in the world soon to come. Our happiness depends on full cooperation with and careful study of His guidelines to health and happiness.

Part of our problem is that our perspective is too limited. We settle for so little when God has so much in mind for us. We need to become experts in demonstrating the beauty and goodness of God's laws in our daily lives.

While serving as a missionary in Japan, I heard Pastor Walter Ogura tell about a young oil salesman who lived in the days of feudal Japan. Passing by an old *soko*, a warehouse, the salesman heard some strange sounds coming from inside. He peered through a crack in the side of the building and was fascinated by what he saw. Some young *samurai* (the feudal knights of Japan) were shooting arrows at targets. The reason they were doing this indoors was that they were just learning to shoot arrows and did not want anyone to see how often they missed the target, let alone the bullseye.

The salesman could not help but burst out with laughter as he saw their amateurish attempts. The samurai heard him laughing and rushed out and grabbed him.

"So, you're laughing at us," they screamed. "Well, if you think you can do better, come and show us. If you can't, we'll fix you for being so disrespectful."

Being on the spot, the salesman had to think quickly. "Honestly," he replied, "I've never shot an arrow in my life.

But I still have every right to laugh at you. You see, shooting arrows isn't my line, but I'm able to do something else very well, so I have a right to laugh when you don't do very well."

While saying this, he took out a coin that, like all the coins of that period, had a small, square hole in it. Holding the coin in front of him, he took a bottle of the lamp oil he was selling and held it at arm's length above his head. Without looking at the bottle, he poured the oil so accurately and in such a light stream that it ran right through the hole in the coin.

He so impressed the young samurai with his skill that they had to let him go.

When I heard Pastor Ogura tell that story, he pointed out that we must not only set our goals for ourselves, but we must be able to hit our targets. Actually, in our Christian lives, God has set the target, the high goals, that are higher than the highest human thought can reach. But He also makes it possible for every one of us to achieve His goals for us.

Of course, God does not expect us to fully reproduce the character of Christ all at once in our lives, any more than we would expect a neophyte samurai to always hit the target with his arrows, or even expect the Japanese oil salesman to accomplish his spectacular stunt the first time he tried it. God gives us grace to grow by. But He does expect us to grow more Christlike each day.

Christ's kind of righteousness, outlined in Matthew 5, so far exceeds anything that we can imagine or achieve by our own physical, mental, or spiritual efforts that there is no possibility of us ever reaching the goals He has set by anything we can do. But what Jesus made crystal clear that glorious day on the mount of blessing is that the humblest, weakest, poorest of us *can* achieve the magnificent results He outlined in His sermon. How? Step by step we follow as He leads up the ladder of Christian progression outlined in the Beatitudes until, by His transforming grace and power, we will be living the kind of lives that characterize the sons and daughters of God.

Chapter 4
Mixing the Price Tags

Writing in the September 23, 1947, *Signs of the Times*, C. L. Paddock told the story of a group of boys, bent on mischief, who broke into a hardware store one night. They did not steal a thing. Their intent was to play a prank. They spent their time changing price tags on many of the articles in the store.

The next morning when the owner came to his shop he found his nails priced at $20 apiece while lawn mowers were only eight cents a pound. Electric fuses were marked at $18 each, but shiny new coaster wagons were selling for just five cents. A popular-brand fountain pen and pencil set was offered for ten cents, but a fly swatter was marked $16. Electric razors were quite a bargain at 25 cents each, whereas a common paring knife would cost $22. The owner was disgusted about the amount of work it would take him to put the right prices on his merchandise again, but he also was amused at the ridiculousness of the situation.

As we look about us in our world today we recognize that someone has stolen in and mixed the price tags. The writer of the article put it this way: "We work and struggle, save and sacrifice, to build up a huge bank account, an estate to leave to someone when we are gone; but in our struggle and sacrifice we entirely neglect some of the worth-while things. God and eternal life are forgotten. We have little or no time for Bible study, for prayer, for worship in His house. Then the end comes suddenly, and we find we had our price tags mixed. . . .

"We spend countless hours and much money in beautifying

our outer selves with cosmetics, clothing, and trimmings and trappings of one kind and another, but we neglect to beautify our inner selves. No one, of course, should be condemned for trying to look his or her best, to be neat and tidy and attractive, but if we spend all our time, energies, and thoughts on the *outside* and have no time for soul culture, for cultivation of a beautiful *inside*, for adding the Christian graces, our price tags are mixed" (page 16).

When Jesus challenges, "Seek ye first the kingdom of God, and his righteousness" (Matthew 6:33), He is doing His best to help us straighten out our priorities, to keep us from getting the price tags mixed. The Sermon on the Mount first explains the steps to becoming citizens of the kingdom as well as outlining true righteousness, with God as its source. Jesus then began to focus on practical aspects of kingdom living.

"In almsgiving, in prayer, in fasting, He said, let nothing be done to attract attention or win praise to self. Give in sincerity, for the benefit of the suffering poor. In prayer, let the soul commune with God. In fasting, go not with the head bowed down, and heart filled with thoughts of self. The heart of the Pharisee is a barren and profitless soil, in which no seeds of divine life can flourish. It is he who yields himself most unreservedly to God that will render Him the most acceptable service. For through fellowship with God men become workers together with Him in presenting His character to humanity" (*The Desire of Ages*, p. 312). What a privilege and what a challenge!

In this section of His sermon Jesus warned against practicing piety in order to gain the attention and praise of those about us. He pointed to several concrete examples of what the Pharisees were doing, such as having a trumpet sounded when giving an offering, praying on the street corners, and filling their prayers with meaningless phrases.

We may be amused when we learn what they were doing and what Jesus told them, but we need to remember that human nature cannot be changed unless God's grace changes it. Today we use other, perhaps more subtle, ways of portraying our righteousness before others.

We need to watch our motives carefully to make sure we are not guilty of sounding trumpets. "Your prayers, your performance of duty, your benevolence, your self-denial, will not be the theme of your thought or conversation. Jesus will be magnified, self will be hidden, and Christ will appear as all in all" (*Thoughts From the Mount of Blessing*, pp. 80, 81).

Nothing to Worry About

Jesus made the point in Matthew 6:24 that we cannot serve two masters. We cannot magnify Christ and ourselves at the same time. It is impossible. Those who love God with all their hearts cannot help but seek first His glory. When they do, the price tags, or priorities, will automatically be sorted out in their lives.

In one of the most challenging, yet assuring, exhortations in His sermon, Jesus advised His audience that they did not need to worry about even their most basic material and physical needs. When we trust and love God supremely, we have nothing to worry about. That does not mean that all our problems will fade away. It does mean that we will trust our Father in heaven to supply those needs that our efforts cannot provide, as He has promised He will.

Many today are turning to materialism, drugs, or other escape mechanisms in an endless search for more and more of that which does not satisfy them when they get it. They spend their time "living it up" but find that doing so does not bring life at its best.

People can become so dominated by the tyranny of things that they are forced to hold garage sales in order to get rid of all the things they do not know what to do with, so that they can have room for more of the same.

A certain man had a wife whose desperate desire was to accumulate things. She kept on pestering him to get something new for her—a new coat, a new car, pearls, furs, baubles without end. Her husband, being a wealthy businessman, was able to gratify her every wish. Finally he bought burial plots for his wife and himself. When selecting the tombstones, he decided on the inscriptions they would bear. "On my wife's," he instructed the engraver, "put 'She Died of Things.' And on mine, write, 'He Died Providing Them for Her.'"

The people gathered on the mount of blessing that day long ago had a living demonstration that they did not need *things* to make them happy. Was anyone ever happier than Jesus? Would you have been, under His circumstances? He had no car, no home, no steady income, no wife, no children, not even a stick of furniture. His family did not understand Him. The fact is that often they opposed what He wanted to do. The highest court in the land condemned Him. He knew that most of the people who were flocking about Him would reject Him in less than a year. He would be forced to spend His third year of ministry among the Gentiles, who would give Him a more favorable reception than did His own people. But after three-and-a-half short years of ministry, one of His own followers would betray Him. He then would suffer a criminal's death and be buried in a borrowed tomb. Yet Jesus was not anxious or worried. He was there doing the will of His Father in heaven and knew that the God who had sent Him to minister at that time and in that place would provide all He needed to accomplish the task He had been sent to do.

Judge Not

Jesus does not command, "Judge not, unless your judgment obviously is a true judgment." Instead He commands, "Do not judge at all." We are so prone to misinterpret what we see and hear that we must avoid condemning others. What we see in others that we do not like ordinarily reflects that which we do not like in ourselves. Therefore, when we judge others, we pass condemnation upon ourselves.

Jesus' advice is to turn our 20/20 critical vision inward so that we see ourselves as God and those about us see us. When we do, we will be so occupied taking care of our own flagrant faults that we will not be able to find time or put forth the effort needed to judge others.

All You Have to Do Is Ask!

Continuing His sermon, Jesus promised that when we ask,

we shall receive (see Matthew 7:7). Of course, as He explained later, this means asking in His name and according to His will. Many have found this interesting acronym in the English translation of verse 7:

Ask
Seek
Knock

Asking involves seeking and knocking. But why must we persist by adding seeking and knocking once we have asked? Mainly because the Father wants us to recognize our need and to be serious about our requests, rather than to be frivolous about what we think we want. He desires to give us all good things, much more than we want, ask for, or even think about, because He loves us so much.

But we still live on a planet embroiled in the constant war that rages between good and evil. For that reason, God is not able to provide for us in the generous way He would like to and will be able to in the new earth when sin in us and around us has been eradicated. Nevertheless, we can place tremendous confidence in the Father's love and concern as expressed by Jesus in His unforgettable sermon: "If you then, who are evil, know how to give good gifts to your children, how much more will the heavenly Father give the Holy Spirit to those who ask him!" (Luke 11:13, RSV).

Because we have our price tags mixed up, we do not always recognize God's loving gifts as those which are best for us. We look at the way He sets before us as difficult and narrow. But the psalmist had the right perspective when he exclaimed, "Thou wilt shew me the path of life: in thy presence is fulness of joy; at thy right hand there are pleasures for evermore" (Psalm 16:11).

Through Christ, God shows us the path of life. On the mount of blessing He declared: "Strait is the gate, and narrow is the way, which leadeth unto life" (Matthew 7:14). In Christ's time, most of the people lived in walled cities that, as far as possible, were set on top of hills or mounds. For defensive purposes the paths leading to them were narrow and difficult to ascend.

"The narrow, upward road leading to home and rest furnished Jesus with an impressive figure of the Christian way. The path which I have set before you, He said, is narrow; the gate is difficult of entrance; for the golden rule excludes all pride and self-seeking. There is, indeed, a wider road; but its end is destruction. If you would climb the path of spiritual life, you must constantly ascend; for it is an upward way. You must go with the few; for the multitude will choose the downward path" (*Thoughts From the Mount of Blessing*, p. 138).

The broad, downward road may seem to us to be the easy way. For that reason most people choose that road. But all along that road are pains and penalties, sorrows and sadness. When we follow the path that appeals to our pride and ambition, we find that it leads to death and destruction. "In the downward road the gateway may be bright with flowers, but thorns are in the path. The light of hope which shines from its entrance fades into the darkness of despair, and the soul who follows that path descends into the shadows of unending night" (*Thoughts From the Mount of Blessing*, p. 139).

But Christ's way, the seemingly narrow way, is the joyful happy way that leads to the kingdom. "All the way up the steep road leading to eternal life are well-springs of joy to refresh the weary. Those who walk in wisdom's ways are, even in tribulation, exceeding joyful; for He whom their soul loveth, walks, invisible, beside them. At each upward step they discern more distinctly the touch of His hand; at every step brighter gleamings of glory from the Unseen fall upon their path; and their songs of praise, reaching ever a higher note, ascend to join the songs of angels before the throne" (*Thoughts From the Mount of Blessing*, p. 140).

The Wise Man put it this way: "The path of the just is as the shining light, that shineth more and more unto the perfect day" (Proverbs 4:18).

The only truly safe and happy way for us to travel is along the path on which we can walk hand in hand with Jesus. When my twin brother and I were about five years old, our parents took us window-shopping on Market Street in San

Francisco. Because the streets were crowded, they insisted that we stay close to them. But five-year-olds like to feel independent, and we were sure that we could get along nicely without holding our parents' hands. Disobeying them, we ran far ahead several times. So they decided to teach us a lesson. The next time we ran on ahead, they stepped into the entryway of a store where they could still see us through the glass, but it was difficult for us to see them. A moment later, we turned to see where they were but could not find them. Two of the widest mouths that ever opened on Market Street gave vent to our feelings of insecurity. I am sure you know what happened next. When our parents revealed themselves to us, we clung to their hands tightly the rest of the way home.

"Our only safety is in walking with Christ, our hand in His, our hearts filled with perfect trust" (*Selected Messages*, bk. 1, p.79).

Building on the Rock

Sometimes we miss the real point of Jesus' parable about the foolish man who built his house on the sand as contrasted with the wise man who built his house on the rock. Jesus used this fascinating illustration to emphasize the point He had just made in His sermon: "Not every one that saith unto me, Lord, Lord, shall enter into the kingdom of heaven; but he that doeth the will of my Father which is in heaven" (Matthew 7:21).

Who is it that builds his or her house on the rock? "Whosoever heareth these sayings of mine, and *doeth* them" (Matthew 7:24, italics supplied). Those who build their house of faith on the sand also *hear* the words, but *do not do them* (see verse 26).

Hearing is important, but for a reason. God's business is not just to interest us with fascinating revelations and intriguing illustrations. He gives us His words of life in order that we may grow spiritually.

Luke adds: "Blessed . . . are those who hear the word of God and *keep* it" (Luke 11:28, RSV, italics supplied). And

44 THE KING HAS COME

James informs us plainly: "Do not merely listen to the word, and so deceive yourselves. Do what it says" (James 1:22, NIV).

The profound truths spoken by the Lord of truth on the mount of Beatitudes are to be used as the foundation of our characters and lives. We are also to treasure and to put into practice "every word that proceedeth out of the mouth of God" (Matthew 4:4). We must take time to study the Word of God daily, for it truly is our "daily bread."

Think for a moment how much time it takes for you and those living with you to prepare and eat your food each day. Be sure you count the time it takes to shop for the food, too, or perhaps even to grow it if you eat out of your garden. But somehow we do not find it too difficult to take that much time for our physical food. Shouldn't we be able to find time for our spiritual food as well? I suppose our doing so depends on our priorities. The following piece taken from the November, 1983 *Worker* gives us some insight into how easy it is for us to put off studying God's Word:

Good morning, Lord!

As soon as I brush my teeth,
I'll study your Word.
Wow! Look at that dirty mirror!
As soon as I brush my teeth,
And clean the mirror
And comb my hair,
I'll study your Word.
Is that the phone?

As soon as I brush my teeth,
Clean the mirror,
Comb my hair,
And answer the phone,
I'll study your Word.
What's that I hear? Oh, it's you, Fido!

As soon as I brush my teeth
And clean the mirror

And comb my hair
And answer the phone
And feed the dog,
I'll study your Word.
Oh, look at the time; I'll be late for work!

As soon as I come back from work
Today, Lord—for sure!

Once we learn to feed ourselves daily on the Bread of Life, we will develop a taste for it and will not want to go one day without it. Then we'll have our price tags straightened out.

Chapter 5
He Touches Us

How thrilling it would have been to live in Palestine and accompany Jesus on His three missionary tours of Galilee! The first tour ended with the Sermon on the Mount late in the spring of A.D. 29. The second took place in the summer and autumn of A.D. 29, concluding with the raising of Jairus's daughter. The third ended about the time of the Passover in A.D. 30. All of the events recorded in Matthew 8 though 10 took place during these three tours, but not in the sequence Matthew presents them.

According to the chronology outlined in volume five of the *SDA Bible Commentary*, the events took place in this sequence:

1. Peter's mother-in-law and other sick healed at Capernaum—8:14-17.
2. The first leper healed—8:2-4.
3. The paralytic lowered through the roof—9:2-8.
4. The call of Matthew—9:9.
5. The centurion's servant healed—8:5-13.
6. Two blind men healed—9:27-31.
7. A dumb demoniac healed—9:32-34.
8. Two who volunteered to become disciples—8:19-22.
9. The storm on the lake—8:18, 23-27.
10. The demoniacs of Gadara—8:28—9:1.
11. Matthew's feast—9:10-13.
12. The invalid woman healed and Jairus's daughter raised—9:18-26.

48 THE KING HAS COME

13. The mission of the twelve—9:36–11:1 (pp. 197, 198).

In these chapters, Jesus demonstrates His power over disease, devils, disaster, and death. Then He empowers His disciples to go and do the same—to "heal the sick, cleanse the lepers, raise the dead, cast out devils" (Matt. 10:8).

Matthew seems impressed with the fact that Jesus touched the leper, touched Peter's mother-in-law's hand, took Jairus's daughter by the hand when He resurrected her, and touched the eyes of the blind men, enabling them to see. He touched them, whatever their needs, whatever their problems—He touched them and made them whole. In touching the leper, Jesus displayed God's intense desire to heal us from sin. His words, "I will; be thou clean," echo through the ages to all who have been infected with the leprosy of sin. His healing touch still cleanses our souls today when we realize our need and come to Him in faith.

How exciting it would have been to watch Jesus reach out, take the hand of Jairus's daughter, and restore the dead girl to life! Shortly before this, Jesus had watched a bereaved mother accompanying the body of her son as the funeral procession wended its way out of the town gate of Nain. Moved with deep compassion, He, the Lifegiver, demonstrated His power to break the bonds of death. Imagine how startled the bystanders were when they saw Jesus step forward, call the young man to life, and restore him to his mother's arms! That was the first time, as far as we know, that He had raised anyone from the dead. Jairus, the ruler of the synagogue at Capernaum, had heard of the great miracle. Now his daughter was dying. He sped to enlist Jesus' help. As Jesus started on His way to Jairus's home, news arrived that the girl had died (see Mark 5:35). Jesus urged Jairus to retain his faith in the Creator's power over death and the grave. When He reached the girl's bedside, He grasped her hand and restored her to life. As Isaiah prophesied, Jesus brought "the oil of joy for mourning" (Isaiah 61:3) into Jairus's home that day.

Wouldn't it have been wonderful to have been present when Jesus touched the eyes of the blind men—to see the light of vision come into their eyes? Imagine Jesus breaking all proscriptions by reaching out and touching the "unclean" flesh of the much-feared leper. How interesting it would have been to hear Jesus address the scribes who criticized Him for forgiving the sins of the paralyzed man: " 'But that you may know that the Son of man has authority on earth to forgive sins'—he said to the paralytic—'I say to you, rise, take up your pallet and go home' " (Mark 2:10, 11, RSV)! What would your feelings have been if you had seen that man roll up his pallet, put it on his shoulders, and walk away with the spring of youth in his steps?

"The paralytic found in Christ healing for both the soul and the body. The spiritual healing was followed by physical restoration. This lesson should not be overlooked. There are today thousands suffering from physical disease, who, like the paralytic, are longing for the message, 'Thy sins are forgiven.' The burden of sin, with its unrest and unsatisfied desires, is the foundation of their maladies. They can find no relief until they come to the Healer of the soul. The peace which He alone can give would impart vigor to the mind, and health to the body" (*The Desire of Ages*, p. 270).

Matthew mentions just a few of Jesus' wonderful miracles of restoration and healing, but he adds: "Jesus went about all the cities and villages, teaching in their synagogues, and preaching the gospel of the kingdom, and healing every sickness and every disease among the people" (Matt. 9:35).

Not only did Jesus come in the ages long past to bind the broken-hearted and to cheer the fainting, but He also comes today to bring us beauty for ashes in our lives. In His love for us Jesus sends the Holy Spirit to change our hearts and lives—to chase away the shadows with the sunshine of His love, to bring beauty for ashes here and now. When we accept Jesus as our personal Saviour and come to know Him as an intimate personal friend, He will fill our everyday lives with the beauty of His love to take the place of the ashes of ugliness and despondency.

The Hem of His Garment

Jesus touched so many with healing, but Matthew 9:20-22

introduces us to a desperate woman who reached out to touch Jesus. Her faith was much stronger than her body. For twelve years she had been suffering from a disease that the doctors were unable to cure. I believe she had been a woman of wealth, but all that she had was spent on trying to find a cure. Now nothing was left but a crippled body and a spark of hope—her faith in Jesus.

She *had* to see Jesus. Painfully she made her way to the seaside. The little fishing boat just then being dragged up on the shore was returning from the Decapolis area. But because a large crowd was pushing around it, there was no way she could get through to Jesus.

She could hear His gentle, lovely voice speaking with the authority of heaven. Then the crowd began to move in toward Capernaum. When Jesus entered Matthew's house, the crowd filled the doorway and the narrow street outside. Suddenly there was a stir in the waiting crowd as they made way for Jairus, the ruler of the synagogue, so that he could plead for Jesus' help.

The crowd pressed around Jesus as He began slowly to make His way on a mission of mercy toward the home where a little girl was dying. The sick woman was desperate. "I must reach Him, I must!" she thought to herself. "Perhaps I can manage to touch the hem of His garment. If I do, I know I will be healed." But she could not push through the crowd in her weakened condition. Just then Jesus began to make His way toward her. Would He pass her by? The dignified lady dropped down into the dust. Everything else was forgotten. She did not care what people thought. Crawling through a forest of knees, she reached out timidly yet hopefully and just managed to touch the hem of Jesus' robe.

An electrifying, shocking thrill came from that touch. She was healed. "In that one touch was concentrated the faith of her life, and instantly her pain and feebleness gave place to the vigor of perfect health" (*The Desire of Ages*, p. 343).

Thrilled and satisfied with the change that took place, the woman retreated back into the crowd, hoping she had been unnoticed. But Someone *had* noticed. Jesus felt the touch of faith and the power that had been drawn from Him.

When He asked, "Who touched me?" Peter, with a snort and a sneer, answered, "What do you mean 'Who touched Me?' The whole crowd is pressing around you. Everybody is trying to touch you." But Jesus could distinguish the touch of faith from the casual contact of the careless throng. While on the way to raise a little girl from the sleep of death, the touch of faith halted Him.

"The wondering crowd that pressed close about Christ realized no accession of vital power. But when the suffering woman put forth her hand to touch Him, believing that she would be made whole, she felt the healing virtue. So in spiritual things. To talk of religion in a casual way, to pray without soul hunger and living faith, avails nothing. A nominal faith in Christ, which accepts Him merely as the Saviour of the world, can never bring healing to the soul. . . . It is not enough to believe *about* Christ; we must believe *in* Him. The only faith that will benefit us is that which embraces Him as a personal Saviour" (*The Desire of Ages*, p. 347).

Although the woman's strong faith led her to reach out and touch the hem of Christ's garment, she then tried to fade away in the crowd. But Christ had much more for her—the blessing of personal testimony and witness that still reaches down to us today. How wonderful it is to touch the hem of His garment! But we are living in a time when we cannot be satisfied with just this blessing.

The strange thing is that when we get a little money, we want more. We taste a bit of delicious food, and we want more. It is human nature to want more. But we receive a mere taste of heaven's infinite blessing and steal away satisfied, as though God has no more to give. What we need to understand is how much God wants to give His people today. How His heart of divine love must hurt when He sees us turn away with so little when He has so much to give us!

Follow-ship

The greatest blessing God can give us is the privilege of witnessing for Jesus. Jesus is not living on earth today. Instead He has appointed His followers to be His representatives. As Matthew 10 discloses, He has commissioned us to carry on His kind of work in the world. Some of His followers do not seem to really understand what He expects them to do.

What He wants us to do is to follow the example He set in His ministry. He turned to Isaiah 61 to explain His mission to His hometown congregation in Nazareth (see Luke 4:16-21): "The Spirit of the Lord God is upon me; because the Lord hath anointed me to preach good tidings unto the meek; he hath sent me to bind up the brokenhearted, to proclaim liberty to the captives, and the opening of the prison to them that are bound."

"To appoint unto them that mourn in Zion, to give unto them beauty for ashes, the oil of joy for mourning, the garment of praise for the spirit of heaviness; that they might be called trees of righteousness, the planting of the Lord, that he might be glorified" (Isaiah 61:1, 3).

He has anointed *us* to preach good tidings and bind up the brokenhearted—to bring them beauty for ashes. That is what the religion of Christ is all about. But sometimes we Seventh-day Adventists get mixed up. We seem to think that it is our business to condemn the world—to bring ashes for beauty, mourning for joy, heaviness instead of praise. Then we wonder why people perceive what we have to offer as something *bitter* rather than something *better*.

But God's remnant people are to be among those called "trees of righteousness" in Isaiah 61:3. We are to be "the planting of the Lord, that he might be glorified." If God has planted His truth and love in our hearts, we will not be gloomy, cranky, critical Christians.

It is true that our message is a solemn one. It involves proclaiming "the acceptable year of the Lord, and the day of vengeance of our God" (Isaiah 61:2). But it also is the message of infinite love, of God's desire that we discover for ourselves and bring to others His happiness, peace, and joy—His beauty for our ashes. How do we accomplish this? By following Jesus' example of ministry. He commissions us as He did

His disciples, to preach the gospel, to heal the sick, and to minister to all in need (see Matthew 10:7, 8).

"There is a work to be done for our churches that few have any idea of. . . . The mission of Christ was to heal the sick, encourage the hopeless, bind up the broken-hearted. This work of restoration is to be carried on among the needy, suffering ones of humanity. God calls not only for your benevolence, but your cheerful countenance, your hopeful words, the grasp of your hand. [He touches others through our hands.] Relieve some of God's afflicted ones. Some are sick, and hope has departed. Bring back the sunlight to them.

"There are souls who have lost their courage; speak to them, pray for them. There are those who need the bread of life. Read to them from the Word of God. There is a soul sickness no balm can reach, no medicine heal. Pray for these, and bring them to Jesus Christ. And in all your work, Christ will be present to make impressions upon human hearts. This is the kind of medical missionary work to be done" (Ellen G. White manuscript 105, 1898).

Notice that she calls this kind of ministry "medical missionary work." Often we entertain a narrow concept of what medical missionary work is. We think that it involves only the kinds of things that doctors, nurses, and other medically-oriented professionals do. But Ellen White's concept is a broad one that includes what each one of us can do. In *The Ministry of Healing* (p. 143), she expands on what is involved, listing the following types of medical missionary service:

1. The poor are to be relieved
2. The sick cared for
3. The sorrowing and bereaved comforted
4. The ignorant instructed
5. The inexperienced counseled
6. Weep with those that weep
7. Rejoice with those that rejoice

Certainly there is something in this list that every one of us can do. For instance, just sending sympathy or congratulation cards or letters fits in categories 6 and 7.

Then the Lord, through Ellen White, promises: "Accompanied by the power of persuasion, the power of prayer, the power of the love of God, this work will not, cannot, be without fruit" (*ibid.*, p. 144).

Medical missionary outreach is to serve especially as an entering wedge. "The right hand is used to open doors through which the body may find entrance. This is the part the medical missionary work is to act. It is to largely prepare the way for the reception of the truth for this time" (*Medical Ministry*, p. 238).

I use what I call the "well-rounded square" model to illustrate why this approach is so effective.

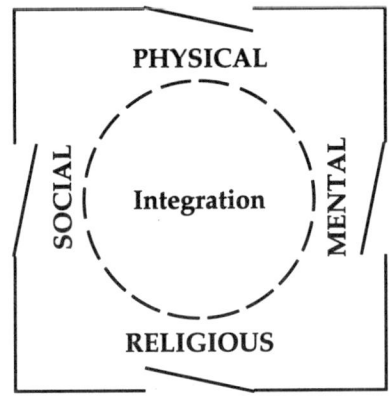

The square represents the four dimensions of personality: the physical, mental, social, and spiritual. These are, of course, thoroughly integrated in the healthy individual and cannot be separated from each other. What affects one affects the others. But for analytical purposes, we show them as four sides of the personality.

We can attempt to reach people for Christ through any of the four dimensions, so there is a door on each side. But some doors are easier to open than others, depending on the individual. The most effective approach involves discovering where the person we are trying to win is most open and responsive. If one approach does not work, it does not make sense to give up without trying the other doors. But so often missionary workers try the spiritual approach, which usually is the most difficult door through which to gain access. When that does not succeed, they turn away, acting as though they have done everything possible, not realizing that there are three other approaches which usually are easier to enter.

With today's tremendous interest in a healthy lifestyle, the time has come for Adventists to use more effectively the medical missionary approach that characterized Christ's ministry. "Christ spent the largest part of His ministry in restoring the suffering and afflicted to health" (*Medical Ministry*, p. 240).

"The world needs today what it needed nineteen hundred years ago—a revelation of Christ. A great work of reform is demanded, and it is only through the grace of Christ that the work of restoration, physical, mental, and spiritual, can be accomplished.

"Christ's method alone will give true success in reaching the people. The Saviour[:]

[1.] mingled with men as one who desired their good.

[2.] He showed His sympathy for them,

[3.] ministered to their needs, and

[4.] won their confidence. Then

[5.] He bade them, 'Follow me' " (*The Ministry of Healing*, p. 143).

Actually, the approach Ellen White calls the medical missionary approach is a full gospel approach, based upon the basic philosophy of Christ's ministry outlined above. The Lord assures us that this is the most effective way to reach out and touch people for Christ. *Medical Ministry* raises the question, "How shall we reveal Christ?" Then it answers, "I know of no better way . . . than to take hold of the medical missionary work in connection with the ministry" (p. 319). The two are never to be separated, but to be blended. This is the method God ordains for us to follow in revealing Christ to the world.

Chapter 6
Pearls of Great Price

The section of Matthew's Gospel beginning with chapter 12:22 and running through chapter 13 forms part of what is known as Jesus' busy day. It probably was no busier than most of His days, but we have been given more information than usual about that particular day in Christ's life. *The Desire of Ages* reports, "It had been an eventful day in the life of Jesus. Beside the Sea of Galilee He had spoken His first parables, by familiar illustrations again explaining to the people the nature of His kingdom and the manner in which it was to be established. . . .

"All day He had been teaching and healing; and as evening came on the crowds still pressed upon Him. Day after day He had ministered to them, scarcely pausing for food or rest. The malicious criticism and misrepresentation with which the Pharisees constantly pursued Him made His labors much more severe and harassing; and now the close of the day found Him . . . utterly wearied" (p. 333).

Two illustrations of the Pharisees' constant harassment are found in Matthew 12:1-14. Both involve Sabbath controversies. Chronologically, both took place before the Sermon on the Mount, not on the "busy day." The Creator and Lord of the Sabbath was being accused by the Pharisees of breaking the Sabbath that He instituted for the benefit and delight of those He had created (see Isaiah 58:13, 14). It was his accusers who had perverted it. "In the days of Christ the Sabbath had become so perverted that its observance reflected the character of selfish and arbitrary men rather than the character of the loving heavenly Father. The rabbis . . . led the people to look upon God as a tyrant, and to think that the observance of the Sabbath, as He required it, made men hardhearted and cruel. It was the work of Christ to clear away these misconceptions. Although the rabbis followed Him with merciless hostility, He did not even appear to conform to their requirements, but went straight forward, keeping the Sabbath according to the law of God" (*The Desire of Ages*, p. 284).

God has placed safeguards around the keeping of the Sabbath in order that we might find the blessing He placed in it and might come apart and commune with Him on this special day. These limits are outlined clearly in the fourth commandment. But keeping the Sabbath as Christ intended and demonstrated should never be confused with a legalistic type of observance. Instead, true Sabbath-keeping comes from hearts so filled with the love of God that they would rather die than displease Him.

The religious leaders of Jesus' day considered Him to be a lawbreaker. If He were here today, many religionists and even some Adventists would call Him a legalist! Why? Because we have come to a strange moment in the history of Christianity when those who love their Lord so much that they seek to bring their lives into conformity to His will are accused of being legalists.

What a travesty of Christlikeness this provides! Those Christians who seek to follow as closely as possible the example that Jesus set often are ridiculed by fellow Christians for being too strict or too rigid in their lifestyle. It is long past time to set the record straight and pinpoint what legalism actually is. The Jewish legalism that Jesus rejected consisted of mere outward conformity to the law. Those legalists kept the Sabbath while putting Christ to death!

In those days, whether a Jew kept the spirit of the law or merely conformed to it externally apparently did not seem to matter to those judging his or her religious life. Conformity to the letter of the law was considered a virtuous fulfillment of duty and was thought to earn the lawkeeper the right to salvation. Jesus valued the law more than did the legalists. He taught His followers to give heed to every jot and tittle. But He pointed out that the strict outward conformity of the Pharisees was worse than worthless because it substituted the letter for the spirit. The fact is that Jesus was even stricter in conforming to the true meaning of the law than were the Pharisees, as His teaching in Matthew 5 illustrates. However, He realized that there was no merit earned toward salvation by obedience to the law. Instead, only conformity resulting from heartfelt gratitude to God serves to indicate that the love of God fills the lives of those completely committed to the Lord. Such obedience has no merit in itself, but signals clearly that the practitioner enjoys a true relationship with God that extends to a commitment to follow God's expressed will in every detail.

The Jews of Jesus' day certainly were orthodox, but orthodoxy is not enough. When the letter of the law is followed strictly, but the spirit of loving obedience is missing, legalism bursts out in full bloom.

And that is what Jesus, and later, Paul, found fault with. Both Jesus and Paul kept the Sabbath conscientiously, but did so out of a loving desire to follow God's will in every respect. Because they did so, the shallowness of legalistic Sabbath-keeping loomed before them as a horrible threat to true Sabbath worship.

Several years ago when I attended a seminary not associated with Seventh-day Adventists, I found it exceedingly difficult to convince my classmates that I believed in salvation by grace through faith alone. They were so indoctrinated with the idea that Adventists were legalists and believed in salvation by works that they did not believe my profession of faith in Christ to be genuine. More than once I was challenged, "You keep the Jewish Sabbath, don't you? That proves you are a legalist." However, one of my more thoughtful teachers said to me one day, "If I had your presuppositions [that the first eleven chapters of Genesis were inspired and literal], I would have to keep the seventh day as Sabbath too."

One argument that seemed to stump those who believed

that I was a legalist because I kept the Sabbath was that I kept the seventh day as a memorial of redemption as well as a memorial of Creation. This had an impact on them because at the time we were studying Karl Barth. He "interprets this covenant between God and man, represented in Sabbath fellowship, as a covenant of grace and redemption to be fulfilled in Christ. Thus the Creation Sabbath speaks prophetically of Christ and must be understood Christologically from the beginning in Genesis 2. . . . The fourth commandment, declares Barth, commands Israel to enter into the rest of divine grace and not to have the slightest trust in the their own work or righteousness before God" (Hans K. LaRondelle, "Contemporary Theologies of the Sabbath," quoted in *The Sabbath in Scripture and History*, ed. Kenneth A. Strand [Washington, D.C.: Review and Herald Publishing Association, 1982], pp. 280, 281).

Although we cannot agree with all the implications that Barth sees in his theology of the Sabbath, we can agree with his position that the Sabbath commandment should be seen "as the comprehensive and fundamental command of all God's commandments, as the sum total of God's covenant of redeeming grace, because only in this commandment are law and gospel fully united."

When fully understood, "the Sabbath is a sign of Christ's power to make us holy. And it is given to all whom Christ makes holy . . . [as] a sign of His sanctifying power" (*The Desire of Ages*, p. 288).

"Come Unto Me"

Because of its underlying significance, the Sabbath is tied in closely with Jesus' invitation in Matthew 11:28: "Come unto me, all ye that labour and are heavy laden, and I will give you rest."

At the end of Jesus' "busy day" He was exhausted. Later He was so weary that He fell asleep in the disciples' fishing boat and was not even aware of one of the worst storms to hit that region. However, as the day was about to end, Jesus forgot His own weariness in the light of the burdens, cares, and perplexities of those pressing about Him. Unable to continue ministering to their needs that day, Jesus concluded His great sermon by the sea in the most gracious words of invitation ever to fall on the ears of human beings. Not only did He bid them to come to Him for rest, but He also added: "Take my yoke upon you, and learn of me; for I am meek and lowly in heart; and ye shall find rest unto your souls. For my yoke is easy, and my burden is light" (Matthew 11:29, 30).

Whoever we are and whatever our burden, Jesus speaks to us, inviting us to lay our heavy loads of care and sorrow on Him. Whatever our anxieties and trials, He is more than willing to listen to our expression of need and open the way for us to find strength to meet our problems. In fact, as He carries more than His share of our load, it becomes light and easy for us.

Have you noticed before the progression in Jesus' words of comfort? Three steps are involved in heeding Christ's invitation:

1. Come (unto Me)
2. Take (My yoke upon you)
3. Learn (of Me).

These three steps bring us freedom from anxiety, guilt, and worry. The first of these is:

1. **Come.** In spite of all malicious propaganda to the contrary, God wants us to be happy. One of my favorite verses is God's promise expressed in David's testimony: "Thou wilt shew me the path of life: in thy presence is fulness of joy; at thy right hand there are pleasures for evermore" (Psalm 16:11). Heaven does everything possible for us to enjoy the inner peace and happiness that our relationship to Jesus brings.

2. **Take.** I like this invitation word better than the word *give*, don't you? In this age of security from the cradle to the grave and the guaranteed annual income, it seems more appealing to *take* than to *give*! What do we take? The text answers, "a yoke." There's the catch—a yoke. We are to take the yoke of service, the yoke of obedience to the law of God.

But Jesus hastens to explain: "My yoke is easy; My burden is light."

When we come to Christ, we exchange yokes. The burden of self-love is a cruel yoke. In comparison, Christ's yoke is much easier. When Christ invites us to take His yoke, He is saying, "Take heaven; take it here and now." That this is so is spelled out in *The Desire of Ages*: "As through Jesus we enter into rest, heaven begins here. We respond to His invitation, Come, learn of Me, and in thus coming we begin the life eternal. . . . The more we know of God, the more intense will be our happiness" (p. 331).

3. **Learn.** Jesus bids us, "Learn of me; for I am meek and lowly of heart." Meekness, as He used the term, is best defined as complete submission to the will of God. Lowliness of heart is to be equated with selflessness. We have to *learn* to be submissive and selfless. But such learning does not come, as many believe, through hammering ourselves into submission. Rather, it comes from learning to know Christ so well and to trust Him so much that we are glad for His way and will to be done in our lives.

Parables of the Kingdom

In His sermon by the sea, Jesus spoke His first parables. "He . . . likened His own work to that of the sower; the development of His kingdom to the growth of the mustard seed and the effect of leaven in the measure of meal. The great final separation of the righteous and the wicked He . . . pictured in the parables of the wheat and tares and the fishing net. The exceeding preciousness of the truths He taught . . . [were] illustrated by the hidden treasure and the pearl of great price" (*The Desire of Ages*, p. 333).

I remember hearing Pastor R. A. Anderson saying time after time, "Salvation is free, but discipleship costs us everything we have." The parables of the treasure hidden in the field and the pearl of great price demonstrate that the joy of salvation is so great that, when we find it, we will be happy to give all we have in order to obtain it.

It was not uncommon in the Palestine of Christ's day to find treasure hidden in a field. There were no bank vaults in those days in which to store treasure. Thefts, robberies, and the pillaging and plundering of invasions took place often. As a consequence, those with valuables to preserve frequently buried them either in the earthen floors of their houses or somewhere in their fields. When those who had buried them were slain in an invasion or carried away into exile, the place where the treasure had been concealed might soon be forgotten. Later, someone plowing such a field would be likely to uncover buried treasure.

Imagine the joy that would follow such a discovery! The problem with the lucky man in the parable was that he did not own the field. He had to sell everything he owned in order to buy the field and make the treasure his. But, because the treasure was worth far more than all he had, he did not hesitate to do so.

Jesus did not tell this story to teach us how to take advantage of our neighbors. His point was that when we find the treasure of the kingdom of heaven we should be more than happy to give all that we have and are for it. The parable also illustrates the tremendous joy that comes from discovering the hidden treasures of the Word of God. The reward we receive as we study is worth far more than the effort it takes to discover the truths that are placed there for us to find. And the effort itself becomes joyful, just as it was with the man in the parable who became so thrilled that he joyfully sold all that he had in order to obtain the treasure.

Matthew 13 also pictures the pearl merchant as gladly selling the precious jewels he had accumulated during his lifetime in order to gain possession of the one spectacularly beautiful and precious pearl of great price. But keep in mind that the salvation offered through Jesus cannot be purchased by anything we do. We cannot earn it. It was blood-bought for us at Calvary by the sacrifice of God's own Son. There was and is no way that any of us could ever pay that kind of price.

What does it mean, then, for the merchantman to sell all that he had in order to buy the magnificent pearl? "This is a beautiful representation of those who appreciate the truth so highly that they give up all they have to come into possession of it. They lay hold by faith of the salvation provided for them at the sacrifice of the only-begotten Son of God" (*Selected Messages*, bk. 1, p. 399).

So the price we pay is *not* the price of our salvation, but *is* the price of our acceptance. Christ paid the great price for salvation, but acceptance and surrender cost us everything we have. The discoverer of the hidden treasure and the pearl merchant who found the one great pearl both gave up *only* what they had. That is all that God expects. But we must be fully detached from self and sin if Christ is to have all there is of us.

"There are some who are seeking, always seeking, for the goodly pearl. But they do not make an entire surrender of their wrong habits. They do not die to self that Christ may live in them. Therefore they do not find the precious pearl. They have not overcome unholy ambition and their love for worldly attractions. They do not lift the cross, and follow Christ in the path of self-denial and self-sacrifice. They never know what it is to have peace and harmony in the soul; for without entire surrender there is no rest, no joy. Almost Christians, yet not fully Christians, they seem near the kingdom of heaven, but they do not enter therein. Almost but not wholly saved means to be not almost but wholly lost" (*Selected Messages*, bk. 1, pp. 399, 400).

It is Jesus who is the flawless Pearl of great price. In Him is gathered all the lustrous glory and beauty of heaven. His purity and righteousness are as unstained as the beautiful white pearl. Every page of the Holy Scriptures shines with the light of the Pearl of great price. In comparison with His precious beauty of life and character, all else fades into insignificance.

We must find the Pearl of great price for ourselves. We must learn to know Jesus—not just know about Him, but come to know Him as our personal Saviour from sin. It is of utmost importance to know what He would do with them if He had our hands and feet. We must learn what He would be

PEARLS OF GREAT PRICE 65

thinking if He had taken over our minds. There is only one way we can learn this and can come to know Him intimately for ourselves and identify fully with Him. That is through careful and consistent daily study of His life, His Word, and through daily meditation upon the beauty of His spotless character.

How can we ever be truly satisfied with anything less when Christ is longing to become our all-in-all—the Pearl of great price enshrined forever in the diadem of our hearts?

Chapter 7
The Bread of Life

"Christ never worked a miracle except to supply a genuine necessity, and every miracle was of a character to lead the people to the tree of life, whose leaves are for the healing of the nations" (*The Desire of Ages*, p. 366).

Two similar miracles, the feeding of five thousand Jews from five loaves and two fishes at Bethsaida and the feeding of four thousand Gentiles from seven loaves and a few fishes in the Decapolis area sometime later, illustrate Ellen White's statement that Jesus' miracles were intended to lead people to the tree of life.

How exciting to have been there when Jesus performed these spectacular miracles and to have tasted that miracle bread! But the bread He provided was merely a token or symbol of something far greater that Jesus longed to share with the multitudes—the Bread of Life. In Jesus' "Bread of Life" sermon in the synagogue at Capernaum, He made it clear that He is "the living bread which came down from heaven" and that "if any man eat of this bread, he shall live for ever." "Whoso eateth my flesh, and drinketh my blood, hath eternal life" (John 6:51, 54). How do we eat of the bread of life? The Lord answers: "The words that I speak unto you, they are spirit, and they are life" (John 6:63).

Ellen White also ties the bread-of-life teaching into the eating-of-the-tree-of-life concept, and adds other fascinating promises: "If the people of God would appreciate His word, we should have a heaven in the church here below. Christians would be eager, hungry, to search the word. They would be anxious for time to compare scripture with scripture and to meditate upon the word. They would be more eager for the light of the word than for the morning paper, magazines, or novels. Their greatest desire would be to eat the flesh and drink the blood of the Son of God. And as a result their lives would be conformed to the principles and promises of the word. Its instruction would be to them as the leaves of the tree of life. It would be in them a well of water, springing up into everlasting life. Refreshing showers of grace would refresh and revive the soul, causing them to forget all toil and weariness. They would be strengthened and encouraged by the words of inspiration" (*Testimonies*, vol. 8, p. 193).

As she suggests, this kind of eating of the Bread of Life takes time and effort. But no more time and effort than it takes to prepare our daily meals. And its benefit goes far beyond anything that can be provided by physical food.

The World's Most Stupid Question

What book makes us WISE when we READ it,
SAVES us when we BELIEVE it,
makes us CHRISTLIKE when we PRACTICE it?

That's not hard—the Bible. But the hard part of the question is, Why, then, don't we read it, believe it, and practice it more than we do?

One time it was my privilege to conduct evangelistic meetings on the island of Okinawa. At that time four Protestant denominations were represented on the island. Seventh-day Adventists were the newest and the smallest of the four. But the saying among the islanders was, "If you really want to know what the Bible teaches, go to the Adventists." We used to have that reputation everywhere. We were known as careful Bible students—but I'm afraid that is not as true today as it once was. It is long past time for a revival among us based on renewed interest in the study of the Bible. How do spiritual renewals and revivals come about? Most of the great revivals of the last two centuries have come as the result of a renewed interest in the study of God's Word. That was true in Bible times too.

In 2 Kings 22:10-19 we read about a spectacular revival that came about in King Josiah's day as a result of renewed interest in the study and reading of long-lost portions of the book of Deuteronomy.

In the same way that God spoke directly through the words of the Book of the Law and through a prophetess to King Josiah, He speaks to us today. What a privilege it is to hold the Word of God in our hands! But, even more, what a privilege it is to read it, study it carefully, and discover for ourselves the truths it contains!

Which leads us to the world's most stupid question. King Zedekiah became a puppet king of the Babylonians. He believed that Jeremiah was a true prophet, but still he would not pay attention to the messages that Jeremiah brought from the Lord.

Speaking of King Zedekiah, Jeremiah 37:2 says: "Neither he, nor his servants, nor the people of the land, did hearken unto the words of the Lord." More than anything else, growing Christians need to know what is God's will for them. King Zedekiah takes the all-time booby prize for one of the most ridiculous questions ever asked. After God, through Jeremiah, had gone to great lengths to let the king know exactly what the military outcome of the Babylonian invasion would be, the skeptical king dared to ask, "Is there any word from the Lord?" (Jeremiah 37:17). Apparently he was hoping that God would change His mind. Patiently the prophet explained once again what the Lord had been telling the king all along—that the Babylonians would take Jerusalem and that it was God's will that they should. But the king and his counselors, who expected help from the Egyptians, would not accept God's word or God's will in the matter.

Many today follow Zedekiah's example in ignoring the clearly expressed will of God, and yet wander about foolishly asking, "Is there any word from the Lord?"

All that those asking this stupid question have to do is pick up their Bibles to find their answer. According to statistics I found some time ago, the King James Version of the Bible contains this many words:

Old Testament	= 592,439 words
New Testament	= 181,253 words
Total	= 773,692 words

So, to the ridiculous question "Is there any word from the Lord?" the answer comes back in thundering statistics. Yes, there is—in fact, God has given us 773,692 words in the Bible.

The problem does not lie with lack of communication on God's part, but with our unwillingness to pay attention. Why should we ever have to wonder what God has to say on a particular question. Through regular, daily eating of the Bread God has sent us from heaven we should be so familiar with God's ways and Word that we will have no trouble understanding His will for us.

Of course, it's not enough to understand fully what God wants us to know. Unless we, by His grace and power, put to work in our personal lives those precious truths He has revealed as a result of careful study, we probably are better off never becoming involved in the search for God's will.

Second Timothy 3:16, 17 lists the reasons why God's Word is so valuable to us. The Bible is given to us in order that we might receive the following great blessings and information:

1. Doctrine
2. Reproof
3. Correction
4. Instruction in righteousness.

The objective of all this is "that the man of God may be complete, equipped for every good work" (RSV).

When we study the Bible, we are not just studying another textbook. Rather, we are allowing God to lead us to a knowledge of what He thinks it most important for us to learn and to put in practice in our lives.

We must feed on the Bread of Life daily. "The mind, the soul, is built up by that on which it feeds; and it rests with us to determine upon what it shall be fed. It is within the power of everyone to choose the topics that shall occupy the thoughts and shape the character" (*Education*, pp. 126, 127).

When we choose to partake of the Bread of Life, we can claim the promise: "He who through the word of God has lived in fellowship with heaven, will find himself at home in heaven's companionship" (*Education*, p. 127).

Eternal Life Begins Now

Have you noticed how Jesus ties the eating of the Bread of Life with receiving eternal life?

In John 5:24, He states: "He that heareth my word, and believeth on him that sent me, hath everlasting life."

In John 6:47, 48, 51, He reiterates: "He that believeth on me hath everlasting life. I am that bread of life." "I am the living bread which came down from heaven: if any man eat of this bread, he shall live for ever "

A few verses later, we read: "Whoso eateth my flesh, and drinketh my blood, hath eternal life" (John 6:54).

Notice that when we partake of the living Bread, we *have* eternal life. It is not just something we look forward to having in the future. "Those who see Christ in His true character, and receive Him into the heart, *have* everlasting life. It is through the Spirit that Christ dwells in us; and the Spirit of God, received into the heart by faith, is the *beginning* of the life eternal" (*The Desire of Ages*, p. 388, italics supplied).

"He that hath the Son hath life" (1 John 5:12). This life begins with the new birth and continues through eternity, as long as Christians have Christ dwelling in them. We receive His life. Thus, it becomes apparent that eternal life should not be equated with immortality, as immortality is bestowed only at the second coming of Christ when "at the last trump . . . we shall be changed" and "this corruptible must put on incorruption, and this mortal must put on immortality" (1 Corinthians 15:52, 53).

Immortality means that we never die again. If we are alive when Christ comes and are given immortality, we never will die. We will have escaped the first death that the Bible calls a "sleep." But eternal life is the opposite of the second death, the "wages of sin" (Romans 6:23). As soon as we accept Christ's life as ours, we are no longer subject to the second death, unless we fall back into a Christless life. As long as we have Christ we have His life—eternal life.

It is up to us to choose life. When J. N. Andrews visited a family living on a farm in Iowa, the young son, who was afraid of preachers, fled to the cornfield and began to hoe corn. After a while, Elder Andrews joined him in his work. Pausing to speak pleasantly to the young man, Andrews asked, "What do you plan to make of yourself?"

"Oh, I hope to earn money so that I can go to school."

"And what then?"

"Then I hope to graduate and become a lawyer."

"And what then?"

"Well, I suppose I'll make some money, build a house, and settle down."

"And what then?"

"Oh, I suppose we'll raise a family and become comfortably well-to-do."

"And what then?"

"I guess I'll grow old."

"And what then?"

"Well, I guess I'll die."

"And what then?"

The young man pondered that question for several days. Then he decided to give his heart to the Lord. He went on to become a great soul winner. In the light of the heaven soon to come, each one of us must take seriously the question, "And what then?"

We can settle that question right now if we choose Jesus, accepting the life that is His as He takes the life that was ours. He paid the price for our salvation, having suffered the second death for us on the cross.

Leaven Instead of the Bread of Heaven

When Jesus warned the disciples against receiving the leaven of the Pharisees and Sadducees (see Matthew 16:6), He had in mind the doctrines or the teachings of these religious leaders (see Matthew 16:12). "As leaven permeates a lump of dough, so the principles a man accepts permeate his life. The comparison is apt indeed, whether the principles be good or evil. The spirit, teachings, and character of the religious leaders, revealed in their hypocrisy, pride, ostentation, and formalism, would inevitably affect the lives of those who esteemed them and complied with their instructions" (*SDA Bible Commentary*, vol. 5, p. 427).

After the Pharisees and Sadducees had joined forces to test Jesus by demanding a sign from Him, Jesus crossed the lake with the disciples to the area near Bethsaida, where the five thousand had been fed. As happened so often, the disciples misunderstood Jesus' warning about the leaven, thinking that He was cautioning them against buying bread from the Pharisees and Sadducees. Because they had left Magdala suddenly to cross the lake, they had only one loaf of bread with them. So the disciples thought Jesus was concerned about where they would go to get bread.

To help set their thinking straight, Jesus reminded them of the miracles of the feeding of the five thousand and the four thousand from just a handful of loaves and fishes, then added: " 'How is it you don't understand that I was not talking to you about bread? But be on your guard against the yeast of the Pharisees and Sadducees.' Then they understood that he was not telling them to guard against the yeast used in bread, but against the teaching of the Pharisees and Sadducees" (Matthew 16:11, 12, NIV).

"As leaven, if left to complete its work, will cause corruption and decay, so does the self-seeking spirit, cherished, work the defilement and ruin of the soul.

"Among the followers of our Lord today, as of old, how widespread is this subtle, deceptive sin! How often our service to Christ, our communion with one another, is marred by the secret desire to exalt self! How ready the thought of self-gratulation, and the longing for human approval! It is the love of self, the desire for an easier way than God has appointed that leads to the substitution of human theories and traditions for the divine precepts" (*The Desire of Ages*, p. 409).

We particularly need this warning as we approach the end of time. Satan will do everything possible to deceive the people of God. False prophets and false teachings are being introduced in the church itself in order to make it as difficult as possible for us to get our regular daily diet of the true Bread of Life. The world about us has turned away from the values taught in the Scriptures, thus exerting subtle pressure on us to do the same. They have turned to such substitutes as the occult, astrology, oriental mysticism, and cults. Both in the church and outside the church, we are surrounded by a growing bombardment of false teachings and satanic lies. Especially now we must heed Jesus' warning against being deceived. Our only safety is in careful, prayerful, daily feeding on the Bread of Life—eating the fruit of the tree of life.

Chapter 8
No Cross, No Crown

Peter must have felt that his up-and-down experience described in Matthew 16 was like jumping back and forth between the height of Mount Hermon and the depths of the Dead Sea. First Peter was blessed by the Lord for his God-given perception that Jesus was the Messiah, the Son of the living God. Then Jesus rebuked him for his Satan-inspired perception that the cross was the last thing Jesus would ever want to experience.

Peter's roller-coaster ride was not his alone. Apparently all of the disciples shared the same feelings, but Peter, of course, was the one who blurted them out. So Jesus gathered the disciples around Him and set the record straight: "If any man will come after me, let him deny himself, and take up his cross, and follow me. For whosoever will save his life shall lose it: and whosoever will lose his life for my sake shall find it. For what is a man profited, if he shall gain the whole world, and lose his own soul? or what shall a man give in exchange for his soul?" (Matthew 16:24-26).

In telling them this, Jesus was not only helping His disciples to keep their priorities straight, but He also was beginning to prepare them to understand that before He could accept the crown of the Messiah He would have to bear the cross of the Saviour.

If you analyze Jesus' words carefully, you will realize that Jesus was not urging us to crucify our true selves. What He wants is for us to crucify the selfish old man of sin in order to let the new man of eternity enjoy the happiness and peace that comes from making Jesus Lord of all in our lives.

Jesus bore His cross all His life, not just on Calvary. Yet He was the happiest person who ever lived. People could mock Him and threaten Him, spit on Him, and even put Him to death. But instead of thinking about Himself, Jesus was concerned about what they were doing to themselves. In His concern for their salvation, He prayed that God would forgive and help them.

Although the cross of Christ, the cross of self-denial, is the happy choice, it is not always the easy one. That's probably why Jesus calls it a cross. But without the cross there can be no crown. Is it strange that the golden scepter that brings us the crown of love is, in reality, Christ's cross? So many who are attracted to Jesus shy away when they see the cross. But Jesus said, "He that taketh not his cross, and followeth after me, is not worthy of me" (Matthew 10:38).

The main reason why so many are hesitant to follow Jesus is that they are afraid to bear the cross. However, Jesus does not take anything away from us that it is in our best interest to retain. When we really love Jesus the cross is not unbearably heavy—in fact, we won't even notice it. Often I've had people say something like this to me: "I want to be a real Christian, but it seems so difficult. There are so many things that we're told not to do. Doing right seems so *hard!*"

As long as we have that attitude, it will be hard. In fact, it will be impossible. We cannot do right without having Christ's spirit of being right. But when we truly love Jesus, we gladly take up our cross and follow Him. The song writer asks: "Must Jesus bear the cross alone, and all the world go free?" Then he answers: "No, there's a cross for every one and there's a cross for me."

Specifically, what is the cross that Jesus asks you to bear? It is the cross of self-denial—the need to give up *anything* that you are allowing to stand between yourself and God. My cross is not necessarily yours, and yours is not mine. Individually we have to sort out for ourselves what it is that blocks our way to Christ and be willing to let Him take it out of the way.

Most likely it is some habit, some characteristic that we know is not good but has been with us so long that we feel we cannot part with it without losing something precious to us. It might be some hatred, some inner feeling that others have wronged us unjustly. But whatever it is, we must realize that it stands between us and full and complete surrender to God's will for our lives. Just admitting that there is something in our lives that we have been trying to excuse and cover up is to take a major step in the process of self-denial.

Naturally, doing so is not pleasant. It is difficult to admit that we've been wrong. It is humbling to our pride to acknowledge that there are things that have such a strong hold on us that we cannot overcome them by our own efforts. That is what Jesus meant when He called on us to crucify self, to take up our cross, to take up His way of thinking and doing.

Our Cross Becomes a Crown

As you probably have often heard, it is not in the truest sense an act of self-denial when we yield all we have and are to God. Actually, we deny ourselves when we don't do this. We forfeit that which brings real happiness and satisfaction now and eternally. When we take up the cross of self-denial, we are amazed to find that what looked to us to be a cross turns out to be a crown—a crown of victory over self and sin— a crown that will be seen by all when Jesus places it on our head as we stand with Him on the sea of glass outside the gates of the New Jerusalem.

Queen Victoria is said to have listened one day to a stirring sermon on the second coming of Christ presented by her chaplain, Dean Farrar. As she was leaving the chapel she grasped his hand, saying, "Oh, I'd so much like to be able to see Jesus come!" Noticing the tears in her eyes, the pastor inquired, "Why is that, your majesty?" The queen answered, "Because I'd like so much to take off my crown and lay it at His feet."

You and I have a crown that we can lay at Jesus' feet right now. It is the crown of the power of choice. The Lord never will force such homage, but if we really want to, we can remove these crowns and lay them at Jesus' feet. In return He'll place another crown on our brow, a crown of love. Only when that crown of love rests securely on our heads, only when real love for Jesus replaces our love for self and He is seen in us, will those about us be attracted to Him in us.

In one of his sermons Moody makes the risen Christ say to Peter, "Go out and find that man that spat in My face and tell him that I forgive him. Go find the man who put the crown of cruel thorns on My brow and tell him that I have a crown ready for him in My kingdom if he will accept salvation. Go find the poor soldier that drove the spear into My side and tell him that I want to make him a soldier of the cross."

No matter how much we have ignored or abused Jesus, He loves us and longs to grant each one of us a crown of life now.

I have heard that in London there is a statue of Christ bearing His cross. It is said that thousands of people pass by each day without even noticing. An inscription underneath reads: "Is it nothing to you, all ye that pass by?" Jesus gladly took up the cross for each of us. What does that mean to us? Are we willing to bear the cross of self-denial for Him?

To live a life of love at home, to develop real love for parents, children, or spouse costs something to self. We have to learn to give of ourselves, to sacrifice time and pleasure, to really work at it. But in the long run we do not count it sacrifice or work or self-discipline. Why? Because love's reward is found in the satisfaction that comes from loving. And this is true in our relationship with Jesus. In *The Ministry of Healing*, speaking of the strongest argument in favor of the gospel—being loving and lovable Christians, Ellen White says: "To live such a life, to exert such an influence, costs at every step effort, self-sacrifice, discipline" (p. 470). Love grows from self-discipline, from learning to put others first and self last. And love for Christ grows from putting Him first. Is it worthwhile to bear this cross of self-denial? The following story demonstrates that it is.

A young singer bore a cross that seemed so heavy she was tempted to give up everything. She had faith. She knew that

God had power to do all things. But she could not believe that He cared enough about her to answer her prayers. Because she didn't believe, she couldn't pray. In her distress she picked up the phone. Almost before her friend could answer, she blurted out, "Something terrible has happened. I'm not a Christian anymore. I've given up everything!"

Then she hung up. But, as she did so, her eyes fell upon a copy of the famous painting of Christ in Gethsemane. The heart she thought so cold began to weep. Through her tears she began singing once again these words:

"Because His love for me led through Gethsemane,
  I know He cares, He cares for me,
Because His plan for me led to the cross of Calvary,
  I know He cares, I know He cares for me."

These words gave the lie to everything she had been thinking and saying. She could not sing them and still doubt that God cared for her. Casting herself at the Master's feet, she wept out a prayer from a heart that knew He cared.

Don't ever think that He does not care. He cares so much that He still bears the scars of Calvary where He denied Himself by giving all He had for us.

The Cross Makes Us Free

The high road to glory is the narrow road of the cross. The transfiguration illustrated this point in a spectacular way. The disciples were discouraged over Jesus' description of His coming suffering. They would be even more discouraged when they would be forced to experience that which to them was unthinkable. To help prepare them for the trauma of the cross, Jesus allowed Peter, James, and John to accompany Him to the mountaintop where He was transfigured. There they heard the voice of God announcing once again, "This is my beloved Son, in whom I am well pleased" (Matthew 17:5). That same announcement had been made at Jesus' baptism. When we are baptized, we may not see the dove descending or hear the Father's voice, but the same assurance is given us—we are God's sons and daughters in whom He is well pleased.

Sons are not slaves. Jesus explained to the disciples that the children of God are free (see Matthew 17:26). John describes an interesting dialogue in which Jesus made this same point. Jesus said to the Jews who partially believed on Him, " 'If you hold to my teaching, you are really my disciples. Then you will know the truth, and the truth will set you free.'

"They answered him, 'We are Abraham's descendants and have never been slaves of anyone. How can you say that we shall be set free?'

"Jesus replied, 'I tell you the truth, everyone who sins is a slave to sin. Now a slave has no permanent place in the family, but a son belongs to it forever. So if the Son sets you free, you will be free indeed' " (John 8:31-36, NIV).

The freedom Jesus offered them not only included freedom from sin but also freedom from death (see John 8:51). Paradoxically, it is only as we accept Christ's cross that we can find true freedom.

Matthew 18 illustrates three aspects of cross-bearing that enable us to become free in Christ:

1. Humility—verses 1-10.
2. Service—verses 11-14.
3. Forgiving others—verses 15-35.

All three involve self-denial, but all lead to glorious freedom from the slavery to self that makes most people's lives almost unbearable. Humility does not lead to a lack of self-esteem. Instead it recognizes that our true value is not in what we are but in what Christ has made possible for us, being sons and daughters of God. Like Jesus, we can bear all kinds of shame and insult that others heap on us because we value ourselves not by what they think of us, but by what God thinks of us. We begin to realize just how much He loves and cares for us.

Jesus' call to us is always a call to service. When He called the disciples by the sea, Jesus invited, "Follow me, and I will make you fishers of men" (Matthew 4:19). He didn't say, "Perhaps you'll become fishers of men." All who truly follow Jesus *will be* fishers of men. We will follow in Jesus' footsteps of service. "We need not go to Nazareth, to Capernaum, or to Bethany, in order to walk in the steps of Jesus. We shall find

His footprints beside the sickbed, in the hovels of poverty, in the crowded alleys of the great city, and in every place where there are human hearts in need of consolation. In doing as Jesus did when on earth, we shall walk in His steps" (*The Desire of Ages*, p. 640).

Forgiving As God Forgives

Getting back to Peter, we find him suggesting to Jesus, with some pride in his evidently magnanimous nature, that Jesus' followers should forgive those who hurt them seven times. How deflated he must have been when Jesus expressed His concern that seven times was far too limited! Instead, the Master told him, we should forgive others seventy times that amount (see Matthew 18:21, 22). Of course, no one is going to keep a record to see if someone has sinned against them 490 times. So the import of Jesus' reply is that forgiveness is not a matter of mathematics: we should always be willing to forgive.

Jesus illustrated our lack of willingness to forgive with a hyperbolic parable. A government official owed his king the staggering sum of 213,840 kilograms of silver. Of course, there was no way he could pay that amount, so, in his kindness, the king forgave the debt. No sooner had the forgiven debtor left the palace than he met a fellow servant who owed him 100 denarii, the equivalent of 389 grams of silver. It was a substantial debt, but ridiculously small in comparison to what he had just been forgiven. Heartlessly, and in spite of the amazing forgiveness he had just received, the official selfishly demanded immediate payment. When it was not forthcoming, he had the debtor thrown into prison. It didn't take long for the king to hear about it. He immediately revoked the forgiveness he had extended, giving the government official the same kind of treatment that he had shown his fellow servant. Not only does this parable teach us why we should forgive others, but it also helps us realize how much we owe God and how unpayable is our debt to Him. Even ten thousand talents are insufficient to describe the measure of God's love and forgiveness.

God's kind of forgiveness is distinguished from our human kind of forgiveness by the fact that when God forgives, He forgets. We may forgive, but we find it difficult to forget. Only as the Holy Spirit enables us to become self-forgetful and completely absorbed in service for others will God's love so fill our hearts that we can forget as well as forgive.

An old man living in one of the Western states truly loved the Lord. He did not have much education, but He loved God so much that he always praised the Lord, especially in church. A doctor who belonged to that church was annoyed with the elderly gentleman for saying "Amen" so much. One day the church member came to the doctor to be treated for a slight illness. The doctor decided that he would do more than treat the man's symptoms—he would attempt to cure him of saying "Amen" so often.

"It'll be a few minutes before I can see you," the doctor told him. "But you take this book on scientific exploration, and I'll tell you what, if you can find anything in this book to say 'Amen' about, just shout it out as loudly as you do in church so that I'll be able to hear you in my office."

The doctor had hardly gotten back through the door before he heard a loud "Amen." Running back, he asked, "Well, what could you find in that book to shout Amen about?"

The elderly church member replied, "Why, I just picked up this book and as soon as I opened it I found out that an expedition to the Western Pacific has discovered a place in the ocean that is seven miles deep. Praise the Lord!"

"What do you care how deep it is?" the doctor asked.

"Why, the Bible says that God casts all our sins into the depths of the sea. There are seven miles of water over them. Praise the Lord!"

But there is something more than seven miles of water covering our sins. They're so covered in Jesus' blood that God Himself cannot see them. When God forgives us, He forgets. His kind of forgiveness is impossible for us to have unless our hearts are filled with His self-forgetful love.

Jesus bids us take up His cross of self-denial and follow Him. But when we reach out in faith to accept His cross, we find instead that He places a crown of love on our heads. With a crown of love resting on our brows, thoughts of love and peace so fill our souls that the love of Christ is reflected from our hearts to all about us. They see that if the Lord can do *that sort of thing* for such people as *us,* He can do the same for them. Then they, too, will want to accept His cross and wear His crown.

Chapter 9
Paying the Fare

The rich young ruler wanted to ride the train, but he didn't want to pay the fare. Many today also want to take the gospel train to its glorious destination, but they hope to ride free—they don't want to have to give up anything in order to go to heaven.

But it doesn't work that way.

It is true that salvation is free. Jesus paid the price of our home in heaven, our golden mansions. There is nothing we can ever do that will earn our salvation. But we have to pay the train fare to get to heaven.

When we get to heaven there will be no expenses. The crowns and harps are given to us even before we enter the gates. When we sit down at the marriage supper of the Lamb we will not pay for the meal or even leave a tip. Travel in the new earth and around the universe will not cost anything. It has all been paid for. But we have to get there, and the trip will cost us something. In fact, as Jesus pointed out to the young ruler, who was unwilling to pay the price, it costs us everything we have. But it's a real bargain even at that. As Ellen White exclaimed after seeing heaven in vision, "Heaven is cheap enough!" Paul called it a "prize."

But perhaps you're thinking, "I can't buy the idea that I have to pay something to get to heaven. Jesus paid it all on Calvary." If so, you're right in one sense: we cannot earn our way to heaven.

To carry out our train illustration a little further, God

provides the railroad. There is no way to get to heaven if we do not board God's train at Calvary station. But the experience of the rich young ruler helps us understand that it costs us something to get on the train.

Jesus' blessing of the children made a tremendous impression on a young man who watched Him. He was attracted by Jesus' love and tenderness. He recognized in Jesus something that was lacking in his own soul. As he came to this realization, he ran down the road after Jesus and stopped Him in order to ask the question, " 'Teacher, what good thing must I do to get eternal life?' " (Matthew 19:16, NIV). There are some today who would respond, "Why, you don't have to do anything; just believe, and eternal life is yours."

But that wasn't Jesus' answer. To the horror of the "cheap grace" proponents of today, Jesus said, " 'If you want to enter life, obey the commandments' " (Matthew 19:17, NIV). And he spelled out several of them so that there would not be any mistake. He particularly referred the young ruler to those commandments that reveal our duty to and the extent of our love for our fellow human beings.

With some pleasure in his achievements, the young man replied, "I've been doing that ever since I was a boy." But he realized that there still was something missing in his experience, so he asked, " 'What do I still lack?' " (Matthew 19:20, NIV).

Then Jesus got right down to the heart of the matter. "Christ looked into the face of the young man, as if reading his life and searching his character. He loved him, and he hungered to give him that peace and grace and joy which would materially change his character. . . .

"The Redeemer longed to create in him that discernment which would enable him to see the necessity of heart devotion and Christian goodness. He longed to see in him a humble and contrite heart, conscious of the supreme love to be given to God, and hiding its lack in the perfection of Christ.

"Jesus saw in this ruler just the help he needed if the young man would become a colaborer with Him in the work of salvation. . . . Christ, seeing into his character, loved him. Love for

Christ was awakening in the ruler's heart; for love begets love. Jesus longed . . . to make him like Himself, a mirror in which the likeness of God would be reflected. He longed to develop the excellence of his character, and sanctify it to the Master's use. If the ruler had then given himself to Christ, he would have grown in the atmosphere of His presence. If he had made this choice, how different would have been his future!" (*The Desire of Ages*, p. 519).

The ruler lacked only one thing. But it was vital. He kept the commandments as well as anyone could without the love of God in his heart. But it is impossible to truly keep the commandments without having them written on the fleshly table of the heart. Jesus helped the young man see this by giving him what appeared to him to be an overwhelming test. He challenged the ruler to sell all of his great possessions and give the proceeds to the poor. He was to choose between earthly treasure and heavenly wealth.

"[Jesus] had shown him the plague spot in his character, and with what deep interest He watched the issue as the young man weighed the question. . . .

". . . His exalted position and his possessions were exerting a subtle influence for evil upon his character. If cherished, they would supplant God in his affections. To keep back little or much from God was to retain that which would lessen his moral strength and efficiency; for if the things of this world are cherished, however uncertain and unworthy they may be, they will become all-absorbing" (*The Desire of Ages*, p. 520).

The young ruler quickly caught the point. He understood the choice he had to make. But he was not willing to make the sacrifice. Because the cost of eternal life seemed so great, he was unwilling to pay the fare. He went away sorrowful. He knew now that his claim to keep the law was a self-deception. Riches were his idol. He did not love God with all his heart.

That's the fare we have to pay if we want to go to heaven—complete surrender of all we have and are to the Lord. Heaven has paid the price of our salvation, but discipleship costs all we have. We cannot serve God and mammon. We have to love God so much that we will not let anything stand between us and service for Him. The ruler was not really saying to God, "I don't want to give you all I possess." He was saying, "No, I can't give you all of me."

Complete surrender of all that we have and are to God means being willing to give up every pet sin or binding habit. Jesus says to us today, "One thing you still lack." If something were not lacking there would be no spiritual poverty in God's church in this time of the latter rain. We lack the spirit of true, selfless love. We may keep the Sabbath and other commandments explicitly. We may tithe and do good to our neighbors, but none of these things have any meaning unless they are prompted entirely by selfless love to God. When our hearts and lives are surrendered completely to God and filled with His love, meaningful obedience and service to others will not be something we put on to cover a cloak of selfishness. Such lives and characters are the natural fruitage of faith and love. Then it is not self that will be seen, but Jesus; not our lives, but His in us.

Riches and Rewards

The Jews of Jesus' day, and that included the disciples, felt that riches came as the reward of piety. Because they held that view, Jesus shocked them when He said, " 'I tell you the truth, it is hard for a rich man to enter the kingdom of heaven. . . . I tell you, it is easier for a camel to go through the eye of a needle than for a rich man to enter the kingdom of God' " (Matthew 19:23, 24, NIV).

Temporal wealth often leads to spiritual poverty because the wealthy are prone to trust in what they have rather than turn to God for spiritual riches. God can only save those who recognize their spiritual destitution (see Matthew 5:3).

Peter expressed the shock of the disciples who looked forward to wealth and position as rewards for choosing to follow the Messiah. "We have left everything to follow you! What then will there be for us?" he wondered.

Jesus did not forthrightly rebuke this selfish question. He realized that many would be attracted to Him because of the reward, even though that is not the purest motive for coming to Him. So He pointed out that the reward of yielding all to Him is far greater than any other reward we can receive. If someone offered you 10,000 percent interest on an investment, you wouldn't believe it, would you. But that's what Jesus assured His disciples they would receive when they gave their all to Him—one hundred times as much, both here and eternally. What a bargain! Heaven is cheap enough!

The Strange Economics of the Kingdom

The disciples were still caught up in the Pharisaic concept that what they did earned them their eternal reward. That is why Jesus told them the parable of the workers in the vineyard. The disciples believed that their reward would be proportionate to their labor. So Jesus pointed out to them that heaven's economics works on a different basis. Because it is impossible for us to achieve heaven by our works, no merit attaches to the amount of work we perform. Our labor merely reveals our love and gratitude for His grace in paying the price of our salvation. Thus, even eleventh-hour Christians have as much right to the kingdom as do those who became Jesus' first disciples. Even those who accept Christ on their deathbeds, although doing so is a most dangerous course to follow, will enjoy as much of the eternal reward as will those who have served Christ all their lives.

"Christ warned the disciples who had been first called to follow Him, lest the same evil [regarding long years of service as entitling them to a greater reward] should be cherished among them. He saw that the weakness, the curse of the church, would be a spirit of self-righteousness. Men would think they could do something toward earning a place in the kingdom of heaven. They would imagine that when they had made certain advancement, the Lord would come in to help them. Thus there would be an abundance of self and little of Jesus. Many who had made a little advancement would be puffed up and think themselves superior to others. They would be eager for flattery, jealous if not thought most important. Against this danger Christ seeks to guard His disciples" (*Christ's Object Lessons*, pp. 400, 401).

Although in heaven's economics our eternal reward is not proportionate to the labor we perform, there is a sense in which our earthly reward reflects that which we do as the grace of Christ makes us more like our self-forgetful Master. Human wisdom equates selfish gain with happiness. But most of us have learned that true happiness comes only in loving, unselfish service to others. As we give we gain, as long as we do not give in order to gain.

One of my favorite persons, Adlai Esteb, tells the unforgettable story of a florist named Henry Penn. At one time he was president of the American Floral Association. "He made his living selling flowers. But he made more than a living out of his business. People came in to buy flowers, and this gave him an opportunity to talk to them—to be kind to them. Many people have problems and buy flowers to settle some difficulty or soothe some heartache. At the side of his desk he had a chair that he called his 'confessional chair.' He said that people came in and sat down there and told him things they ought to have told their preacher. You know, we do try to 'say it with flowers.'

"Well, one day three little children came in and said, 'We want to get some flowers.' He showed them some flowers, and then they said, 'No, those won't do. We want yellow flowers.' So he showed them some yellow flowers. Then the children shook their heads and said, 'No, those aren't good enough.' Then he said, 'Well, who are these for that those beautiful flowers aren't good enough? Come over and sit down and tell me all about it.' Then the little spokesman answered, 'These are for Mickey.'

" 'But who is Mickey?' asked the florist.

" 'Well, Mickey was our . . . playmate, and yesterday a truck ran over him and killed him. This morning the kids on our street got together, and we have taken up a collection of eighteen cents to buy flowers for the funeral.'

" 'Now that is different,' said Mr. Penn. 'I understand now. Come with me and we'll find some flowers. But you say that they must be *yellow* flowers. Why must they be yellow?' Thinking, no doubt, of so many other beautiful colors.

"The little lad was quick to answer, ' 'Cause Mickey always wore a yellow sweater, and we think Mickey would like it better that way.'

"Mr. Penn replied, 'Now I understand perfectly. Come with me.' He then took them to a special room and showed them a great bank of yellow rosebuds. 'How would those flowers do?' he asked.

"The children exclaimed, 'Wonderful! Those would be wonderful, Mr. Penn.' Then he replied, 'Well, I happen to have a special on those rosebuds today for only eighteen cents.'

" 'Oh,' they said, 'we'll take them, Mr. Penn. Those would be swell.'

"He asked, 'Where shall I send them?'

"The children talked to one another a moment, then the little spokesman said, 'Please, Mr. Penn, we'd rather take them with us. We think Mickey would like it better that way.'

"So he filled their arms full of beautiful yellow rosebuds—a clear loss of many dollars to Mr. Penn, but a clear gain of an ecstasy that lasted for days. Who can say that Mr. Penn did not reap a far richer reward for being kind than mountains of gold could ever buy?" (Adlai Esteb, *Kindle Kindness* [Hagerstown, Md.: Review and Herald Publishing Association, 1965], pp. 6-9. Used by permission).

The rich young ruler, who was much poorer spiritually than he realized, could have had the kind of riches Mr. Penn so abundantly received if that young man had been willing to deny himself and take up the glorious cross of love and service. He apparently had a good grasp of secular economics, but he allowed this to so distort his understanding of heaven's economics that he did not realize how much he actually was giving up to retain that which has no eternal significance.

The Day They Welcomed the King

Recognizing that the cross must precede the crown, Jesus, knowing that His time had come (see John 12:23), precipitated the final events of His life by sending two of his disciples to request a donkey and her colt for His use in His triumphal entry. The colt had never been ridden before. By riding it, Jesus fulfilled the prophecy of the coming of the Messiah recorded in Zechariah 9:9, thus purposely announcing His role as rightful King of Israel.

This is the only time in the Gospels that we have a record that Jesus rode something. Prior to this He always had traveled on foot. In riding the colt, "Christ was following the Jewish custom for a royal entry. The animal on which He rode was that ridden by the kings of Israel" (*The Desire of Ages*, p. 570).

To me, it is fascinating that Jesus began His triumphal entry into Jerusalem from the Mount of Olives. When He next touches earth, He will come as King of kings when the Holy City descends. As His feet touch the Mount of Olives, it will divide into a vast plain on which the New Jerusalem will rest (see Zechariah 14:4; Revelation 21:2).

For the first time in His life Jesus accepted the rightful homage of the multitudes and His disciples who for so long had wanted to make Him King. In doing so, He stirred up the jealousy of His enemies so much that they became more determined than ever to put Him to death as soon as possible.

"Never before in His earthly life had Jesus permitted such a demonstration. He clearly foresaw the result. It would bring Him to the cross. But it was His purpose thus publicly to present Himself as the Redeemer. He desired to call attention to the sacrifice that was to crown His mission to a fallen world." (*The Desire of Ages*, p. 571).

Even then, as Zechariah had predicted, the coming of the King was meek or lowly when compared to the unprecedented glory He could have manifested and that will be manifested when He returns to earth.

All around Jesus during His triumphal entry "were the glorious trophies of His labors of love for sinful man. There were the captives whom He had rescued from Satan's power, praising God for their deliverance. The blind whom He had restored to sight were *leading the way*. The dumb whose tongues He had loosed *shouted the loudest hosannas*. The cripples whom He had healed *bounded with joy*, and were the most active in breaking the palm branches and waving them before the Saviour. Widows and orphans were exalting the name of Jesus for His works of mercy to them. The lepers whom He had cleansed spread their *untainted* garments in His path, and hailed Him as the King of glory. Those whom His voice had awakened from the sleep of death were in that throng. Lazarus, whose body had seen corruption in the grave, but who now rejoiced in the strength of glorious manhood, led the beast on which the Saviour rode" (*The Desire of Ages*, p. 572, italics supplied).

What a glorious scene! Yet it was the path to Calvary. Jesus gladly took up His cross in order to pay the price of our salvation.

Today the gospel train stands waiting for its passengers. Its destination is the New Jerusalem. But we must pay the fare the rich young ruler thought was too high. We must take up our crosses of self-denial and give all we have and are to the One who gave so much more for us.

Chapter 10
No Gate-Crashers in Heaven

Switching metaphors from the last chapter, we turn to Jesus' parable of the wedding banquet in Matthew 22:1-14. Here we find that we cannot attend the marriage supper of the Lamb unless we are willing to allow the Lord to clothe us with the special wedding garment He has prepared for us. Among those rounded up to attend the marriage feast in Christ's parable was a man who did not think he needed a wedding garment, but this will not be true at the wedding feast in heaven. All the guests allowed in will have to be wearing the wedding garment—Christ's robe of righteousness. But before we can put His garment on, we must be willing to let Him take off our filthy garments of sin.

I know you have felt the horror that comes with a sense of sin. How terrible it is! It makes you disgusted with yourself. You have wanted to do right, but you have ended up doing wrong. As a consequence, you are ashamed and disgusted. But do you know who is making you feel disgusted? You could answer that it is both the Holy Spirit and Satan—and you would be right. The Holy Spirit points out sin, but He doesn't want us to become discouraged by it. It is Satan who tries to discourage us.

However, when you feel a sense of discouragement, read these words: " 'Remove the filthy garments from him. . . . Behold, I have taken your iniquity away from you, and I will clothe you with rich apparel' " (Zechariah 3:4, RSV). Of all people, it was the high priest, Joshua, who was clothed in the filthy garments of sin. But, of course, in Zechariah's vision, he represented all of us at that point in his experience. In Joshua's case Satan apparently ran out of arguments. He had been pointing out Joshua's sinfulness, and was still there. But what could he say now that the filthy garments had been taken away and replaced by the robe of Christ's righteousness?

From this experience we see that putting on the wedding garment of justification involves two practical accomplishments:

1. It destroys the guilt of past sins. Joshua's filthy garments were removed.

2. It includes the new-birth experience. Joshua was given new garments.

"The spotless robe of Christ's righteousness is placed upon the tried, tempted, faithful children of God. The despised remnant are clothed in glorious apparel" (*Prophets and Kings*, p. 591).

"Through faith in His name He imputes unto us His righteousness, and it becomes a living principle in our life" (*That I May Know Him*, p. 302).

A Crown of Love

Perhaps we have the idea that the wedding garment, the robe of Christ's righteousness, is all that we need. But in the vision of Joshua being clothed with the garments of righteousness in place of his filthy garments of sin, there was something more that was needed. Zechariah himself recognized what was missing and urged, " 'Put a clean turban on his head.' So they put a clean turban on his head" (Zechariah 3:5, NIV). The turban the priest wore bore the inscription, "Holiness to the Lord" (Exodus 28:36).

Justification does not stand alone in our Christian experience. Romans 6:17-22 and 1 Thessalonians 4:1-3 indicate clearly that there must be an accompanying sanctification. "Sanctification is a state of holiness, without and within, being holy and without reserve the Lord's, not in form, but in truth.

Every impurity of thought, every lustful passion, separates the soul from God; for Christ can never put His robe of righteousness upon a sinner, to hide his deformity. . . . There must be a progressive work of triumph over evil, of sympathy with good, a reflection of the character of Jesus. . . .

"Conformity to the likeness of Christ's character, overcoming all sin and temptation, walking in the fear of God, setting the Lord continually before us, will bring peace and joy on earth, and ensure us pure happiness in heaven" (*Our High Calling*, p. 214).

The Hebrew word translated *fair* that modifies *mitre* (turban) in Zechariah 3:5 means "to be clean, to be pure," or "to be pronounced clean or pure." The Lord plans that the minds of His people will be fully surrendered to the indwelling of the Holy Spirit.

We often fail to realize the extent of what God can do for us. He writes His laws on the table of our minds. He takes away our inclination to sin. *The Desire of Ages* tells us that He gives us power to overcome "all hereditary and cultivated tendencies to evil" (p. 671). In their place He writes on our mind, "Holiness to the Lord."

When we accept His cross of self-denial, He places a crown of love on our heads. Then we are able to think His thoughts after Him.

The Great Commandment

Jesus made it clear to the Pharisees and Sadducees, who were trying to find some reason for condemning Him to death for violating God's laws, that wearing the crown of love means having God's laws of love written in our hearts and minds. Jesus was teaching in the temple on the Tuesday before the crucifixion. Both the Pharisees and Sadducees kept sending their representatives to try to trap Him into saying or doing something that they could use as evidence against Him. One group of insincere "spies," as Luke calls them (see Luke 20:20), tried to trap Jesus on the question of whether or not they should pay tribute to Caesar. Then the Sadducees raised one of their stock questions about the resurrection. It was one they had used to embarrass the Pharisees because the latter seemed unable to find a plausible answer. Jesus had no trouble in answering the stickler. He silenced the representatives of the Sadducees by pointing out that they were wrong in their assumptions because they were not very keen students of the Scriptures.

Next, the Pharisees took another turn at trying to trap Jesus. They sent a rather sincere young lawyer to ask Him, "Master, which is the great commandment in the law?" (Matthew 22:37). In response Jesus made it clear, by quoting Deuteronomy 6:5 and Leviticus 19:18, that one great principle underlies the entire law—love. Unless we wear Christ's crown of love, nothing we do can conform to the basic principle that makes God's law a law of love. It is impossible to keep the law without genuine love for God and for those about us.

God longs for us to experience genuine love because it is basic to our entire Christian relationship. In Romans 13:10 Paul tells us that "love is the fulfilling of the law."

Henry Drummond had great talents in science and mathematics, but as a young man he entered the ministry in Scotland. While at the peak of his abilities and in the full ardor of his love for Christ, he prepared a sermon on 1 Corinthians 13 entitled "The Greatest Thing in the World." The sermon was such a masterpiece that it soon was printed and circulated throughout the Christian world. In this masterful sermon, Drummond asked, "Why is love greater than faith?" Then answered, "Because the end is greater than the means." He went on to illustrate how love is the fulfilling of the law, pointing out that you can say to a man who loves his wife with all tenderness, "You are at liberty to beat her, hurt her, kill her if you want to." He just naturally *won't want to.* Drummond added that if we really love, it is preposterous to say to us, "Do not kill." It is insulting to suggest, "Do not steal." It is unnecessary to beg, "Please do not bear false witness against your neighbor." And the last thing we would want to do is to covet that which is our neighbors'.

Yet somehow, and very gradually over the years, Drummond's interest in a liberal, scientific approach to religion led him away from a sense of personal commitment to Christ. One day it came as a shock to him to realize that he had drifted away from the simple, loving faith he had once known. The resulting turmoil in his life was aggravated by the news that he had been diagnosed as having an incurable illness.

To his friend, Sir William Dawson, Henry Drummond announced, "I'm going back to the Bible." To him that meant restudying 1 Corinthians 13. As he reread his own sermon "The Greatest Thing in the World" he fell in love with Christ again. The sermon he had written in his early days in the ministry saved his spiritual life. In the few remaining months he was allowed to live he declared, "Ten minutes spent in Christ's company every morning, aye, two minutes, if it be face to Face and heart to Heart, will change the whole day."

Love *is* the greatest thing in the world. It is the very essence of Christian thought and life. Love is the Decalogue in action. It is the basis of the golden rule. In fact, you can reduce the entire Bible to one word, "love."

Jesus made it clear to the young lawyer and to all who were listening that there are only two legitimate objects of love. We can *like* antiques and apples, but we cannot really *love* them. As Christians our first and foremost love is directed to God. Next, we are to love our neighbors as ourselves. But it is not something we can develop on our own. "Love is a precious gift, which we receive from Jesus" (*The Ministry of Healing*, p. 358).

Love is received as the fruit of the Holy Spirit. Have you noticed that nine gifts are mentioned in Galatians 5:22, 23. But it is love that *is* the gift of the Spirit. All the other gifts center in and lead to love.

Love is not passive. It demands and always leads to specific action. Paul states: "Christ's love compels us" (2 Corinthians 5:14, NIV). It is the motivating force in the Christian's life. It compels Christians to loving, self-sacrificing service. When we love Jesus we have to do something about it. And that something demonstrates our love for Him and is evidenced in loving, kind deeds to those around us.

Love Sometimes Has to Rebuke

In the light of what we have just discussed about God's love and Christian love, how do we explain what Jesus did next? He concluded His last discourse in the temple by pronouncing eight woes on the scribes and Pharisees, denouncing them as "hypocrites" (Matthew 23:13), "blind guides" (Matthew 23:16), "fools" (Matthew 23:17), "whited sepulchres" (Matthew 23:27), and "serpents" and "vipers" (Matthew 23:33). How out of character such words seem falling from the lips of our loving Lord!

But we need to keep in mind the words of the Revelator, who quotes Jesus as saying, "As many as I love, I rebuke and chasten" (Revelation 3:19). Wasn't He going a little too far, though, in His rebuke of the priests and rulers? Why did Jesus do something that seemed so out of character for Him?

We turn to *The Desire of Ages* for a detailed explanation: "It was the last day of Christ's teaching in the temple. . . . There stood the young Galilean, bearing no earthly honor or royal badge. Surrounding Him were priests in their rich apparel, rulers with robes and badges significant of their exalted station, and scribes with scrolls in their hands, to which they made frequent reference. Jesus stood calmly before them, with the dignity of a king. As one invested with the authority of heaven, He looked unflinchingly upon His adversaries, who had rejected and despised His teachings, and who thirsted for His life. . . . He had set before these leaders their real condition, and the retribution sure to follow persistence in their evil deeds. The warning had been faithfully given. Yet another work remained for Christ to do. Another purpose was still to be accomplished.

"The interest of the people in Christ and His work had steadily increased. They were charmed with His teaching, but they were also greatly perplexed. They had respected the priests and rabbis for their intelligence and apparent piety. In all religious matters they had ever yielded implicit obedience to their authority. Yet they now saw these men trying to cast discredit upon Jesus. . . . They marveled that the rulers would not believe on Jesus, when His teachings were so plain and simple. They themselves knew not what course to take. . . .

"In the parables which Christ had spoken, it was His purpose both to warn the rulers and to instruct the people who were willing to be taught. But there was need to speak yet more plainly. Through their reverence for tradition and their blind faith in a corrupt priesthood, the people were enslaved. These chains Christ must break. The character of the priests, rulers, and Pharisees must be more fully exposed" (pp. 610-612).

Because the Pharisees themselves did not follow their own teachings, Jesus pointed out again and again that they were "hypocrites" and "blind guides" who could not be trusted. Admittedly, Jesus used the shock treatment, but many who were there would never forget that day when Jesus called a spade a spade. That included some of the priests and rulers who later joined the Christian church (see Acts 6:7).

Jesus' main burden in His last discourse in the temple was to make it clear that there would be no gate-crashers in heaven. No matter what the Pharisees believed, taught, or did, the only way to heaven was the way God provided—Jesus the Way, the Truth, and the Life. Their useless restrictions were making God's religion a burden. They went to such extremes as forcing the people to strain the water they used in order to keep them from inadvertently ingesting a tiny insect because they would be guilty of breaking the laws against eating unclean animals. At the same time that they were spending vast sums of money on beautifying the tombs of the dead prophets, they were plotting to put to death the greatest of the prophets. Most of all, they were deceiving themselves as well as the people into thinking that they were earning their way into the kingdom.

Even though Jesus had minced no words in keenly denouncing their sins, He did not manifest anger toward those plotting against Him. He was concerned about their salvation as well as that of the multitudes they were deceiving. He rebuked them with tears in His voice.

"Divine pity marked the countenance of the Son of God as He cast one lingering look upon the temple and then upon His hearers. In a voice choked by deep anguish of heart and bitter tears He exclaimed, 'O Jerusalem, Jerusalem, thou that killest the prophets, and stonest them which are sent unto thee, how often would I have gathered thy children together, even as a hen gathereth her chickens under her wings, and ye would not!' This is the separation struggle. In the lamentation of Christ the very heart of God is pouring itself forth. It is the mysterious farewell of the long-suffering love of the Deity.

"Pharisees and Sadducees were alike silenced. Jesus summoned the disciples, and prepared to leave the temple, not as one defeated and forced from the presence of His adversaries, but as one whose work was accomplished. He retired a victor from the contest" (*The Desire of Ages*, p. 620).

Chapter 11
Seven Parables of Preparedness

The tears in Jesus' eyes were real the day He wept over Jerusalem. It was the most triumphant day of His life. The crowds about Him were crying out, "Hosanna to the Son of David: Blessed is He that cometh in the name of the Lord; Hosanna in the highest!" (Matthew 21:9).

The Son of God's people were about to crucify Him—but how much He loved them! As He rode over the brow of the Mount of Olives and looked down upon Jerusalem, Jesus began to weep. Probably He still sheds tears when He surveys His people on earth. In heaven, surrounded with all the unimaginable beauties of a perfect world, His thoughts are concentrated upon His people on earth. Tears of disappointment may be flowing down His cheeks right now. He wants so much to come and receive us unto Himself so that we can be with Him where He is.

Yet we are so taken up with the cares, anxieties, and interests of life in this imperfect world that at times we seem indifferent to the *thrilling* promise of Christ's return.

I do not doubt at all that the same Jesus who wept over Jerusalem, in His disappointment over our lack of readiness and willingness to go home with Him, turns to the Father with tears in His eyes and His voice. "Father," He sobs, "what is the matter with My people on earth? Father, don't they *want* to come home?"

What about it? Don't we *want* to go home?

It's Later Than It Has Ever Been

Actually, instead of singing the hymn we sometimes sing, "It's Almost Time for the Lord to Come," we ought to sing, "It's *Long Past* Time for the Lord to Come."

What time is it? It's later than it's ever been! When I was a boy living in San Francisco, my folks had an old bronze clock that was shaped like an early California forty-niner. He was carrying a pick in one hand and a pan used for panning gold in the other. The miner's clock was in the room where my twin brother and I slept. Sometimes at night the clanging of the clock as it struck the hour would wake us up. But that clock had a bad habit. It didn't know when to quit. I remember several occasions when it struck 15 or 16 o'clock!

Another little boy must have had a clock like that in his room, for one night he heard it strike fourteen times. Becoming excited, he ran into his parents' room, screaming, "Mommy, Daddy, come quick, come quick! It's later than it's ever been!" That's what time it is on the clock of prophecy. It's later than it's ever been. As Paul advises in Romans 13:11, 12, it is high time to awake out of our sleep and get ready for Christ to come.

"The End Is Near"

Few in the West had ever heard of Chernobyl until April 26, 1986. Early that morning an explosion blew the roof off the nuclear plant's Number 4 reactor. In less than three seconds another explosion sent a burst of radioactive gases shooting half a mile into the sky. Radiation emissions from the explosion soon spread over Northern Europe as well as the Soviet Union, finally reaching as far away as the United States. The world's worst nuclear accident killed at least thirty people, leaving many more suffering from radiation damage. Hundreds of square miles were contaminated, inflicting medical and environmental hazards that may continue for generations.

SEVEN PARABLES OF PREPAREDNESS 105

This terrifying incident awakened the world anew to the threat of the nuclear "sword of Damocles" hanging over its head. As a result many hearts continue to faint "for fear, and for looking after those things which are coming on the earth" (Luke 21:26). Certainly the signs of the times on the roadposts to heaven indicate that we are almost there.

Another Bible description of the last days is found in Revelation 11:18: "The nations were angry, and thy wrath is come, and the time of the dead, that they should be judged, and that thou shouldest give reward unto thy servants the prophets, and to the saints, and them that fear thy name, small and great; and shouldest destroy them which destroy the earth." In this age of unprecedented buildup of nuclear weapons and the environmental hazards imposed by pollution of all kinds, we certainly have arrived at a time when human beings are capable of destroying the earth. Scientists warn that unless something drastic is done soon, the earth will not last long.

No wonder, then, that thinking people everywhere, especially those attuned to Bible prophecy, are convinced that we are living in the end of time and that Christ is soon to return.

The unprecedented *intensity* in the increase of the traditional signs of Christ's return found in Matthew 24 lead many today to realize that it will not be long before the little cloud, about half the size of a man's hand, heralds the great day when Jesus returns. Notice these indications of intensity:

Wars—the most devastating of all time mark this century.

Famines—as many as 250 million people are starving today. It is estimated that by the year 2,000, one-fifth of the world's population will be caught in the throes of hunger.

Pestilences—the cancer storm and AIDS more than fill the bill.

Earthquakes—on July 28, 1976 two massive earthquakes ripped Tangshan, China, leaving 750,000 people dead in its ruins. It was the greatest earthquake disaster in recorded history. And killer earthquakes continue.

Yet Jesus predicted that these signs of the times would be neither the most significant nor the ultimate ones (see Matthew 24:8). The most consequential and the truly ultimate signs focus on the *church* rather than the world. We often apply the words of Matthew 24:12, "And because iniquity shall abound, the love of many shall wax cold," to the world. But if you study carefully verses 9 to 11, you will realize that Jesus is talking about the *church* at this point in his discourse; thus His words must in particular apply to the remnant church.

Verse 14 indicates the fulfillment of the special mission delegated to those who are given the responsibility of proclaiming the three angels' messages. In this verse we discover the ultimate sign. When the gospel is "preached in all the world for a witness unto all nations," Jesus says, "then shall the end come."

What He predicted about the condition of the remnant church in verse 12 *is* taking place. Among those commissioned to witness to the world about Jesus' soon coming, the love of many *has* waxed cold. We do not have to document the gruesome details. They are visible even to the casual onlooker.

Yet, in the midst of the frigid unresponsiveness of many of God's people will be seen the blazing fire of the latter rain. It will spread "like fire in the stubble" (Ellen White, *Review and Herald*, December 15, 1885, p. 1). "Light will be communicated to *every* city and town" (*Evangelism*, p. 694, italics supplied).

Study carefully the thrilling promises and the challenge contained in these words:

"The end is near! God calls upon the church to set in order the things that remain. Workers together with God, you are empowered by the Lord to take others with you into the kingdom. You are to be God's living agents, channels of light to the world, and round about you are angels of heaven with their commission from Christ to sustain, strengthen, and uphold you in working for the salvation of souls.

"I appeal to the churches in every conference: Stand out separate and distinct from the world—in the world, but not of it, reflecting the bright beams of the Sun of Righteousness, being pure, holy, and undefiled, and in faith carrying light into all the highways and byways of the earth. . . .

"If you would go forth to do Christ's work, angels of God would open the way before you, preparing hearts to receive the gospel. Were every one of you a living missionary, the message for this time would speedily be proclaimed in all countries, to every people and nation and tongue. This is the work that must be done before Christ shall come in power and great glory. I call upon the church to pray earnestly that you may understand your responsibilities. Are you individually laborers together with God? If not, why not? When do you mean to do your heaven-appointed work?" (*Testimonies*, vol. 6, p. 436-438).

Preparation for His Coming

Many Bible students are so taken up with the *signs* of Christ's coming when they study Jesus' prophecy in Matthew 24 and 25 that they fail to see what Jesus was trying to communicate. When you stop and analyze it, the interest in the signs of His coming as expressed in the questions of the disciples is really only the launching pad for Jesus' discourse on the Mount of Olives. By studying the entire context in Matthew 24 and 25, you will discover that only verses 4 through 31 of chapter 24 specifically deal with the outline of the signs of the times. That's twenty-eight verses in all devoted to this phase of the topic. Even here the emphasis is on the importance of not being deceived by Satan's last-day deceptions rather than being able to tell *when* Christ will return.

But the sixty-six verses which follow (more than twice the number than in the previous section) indicate what must be accomplished in order to *be ready*. In other words, the emphasis in Christ's discourse is not so much on the signs, which we so often emphasize, but on being ready so that He may come.

As He so often did when He wanted people to remember and repeat what He taught, Jesus put these teachings in parable form. Matthew 24:32—25:46 consists of seven parables of preparedness. Jesus challenges us to "watch and be ready." In these verses He explains more clearly than anywhere else in the Bible what it means to be ready. His teaching is summarized in the chart that follows:

Parables of Preparedness	Meaning of *Watch*	Attitude
24:32-35—Fig tree	Nearness	Awareness
24:36-42—As in the days of Noah	Unexpectedness	Interest, concern
24:43, 44—Thief in the night	Readiness	Watchfulness
24:45-51—Two types of servants	Responsibility	Faithfulness
25:1-13—Ten virgins	Spiritual responsibility	Consecration, dedication
25:14-30—Talents	Diligence (Stewardship)	Loving anxiety to share
25:31-46—Sheep and goats	Love	As Christ loved

In Chuck Yeager's autobiography, the well-known war hero and test pilot who first broke the sound barrier tells about his flight across the Atlantic with famous woman pilot Jackie Cochran to visit the Soviet Union. Before they set out they had received permission from Air Force Chief of Staff General Tommy White to make stops at various Air Force installations for refueling and service. General White had sent letters ahead to base commanders along the way.

One of their first stops was to be at Presque Isle, Maine,

around two in the morning. They were almost out of fuel as they approached the field. But when they got the tower on the radio, permission to land was refused. Yeager told them they had permission from General White, but the tower personnel simply said, "So does Lana Turner."

They argued over the radio for a while. Finally Yeager told them that this was an emergency, and they were going to have to let him land as they were about to run out of fuel. The tower threatened to turn off the runway lights. But they went ahead and landed. As soon as their plane stopped rolling, it was surrounded by Air Force police who escorted them under guard to base operations. Finally the base commander arrived.

" 'You people will leave immediately,' he said. 'This base is closed to all civilian traffic.' "

Jackie Cochran asked for permission to make a phone call on her credit card, even though it was 2:30 A.M. She got General White at his home in Washington and explained the situation to him. He asked to speak to the base commander. When she handed the telephone to the colonel, he snapped to attention, muttering "Yes, sir" over and over as he talked long distance to the Chief of Staff.

When he hung up, he said to Jackie, " 'Miss Cochran, you may have anything you need or want, including this air base.' "

The colonel had *not* read his mail. He was *unaware* that very important guests were scheduled to land at his base. Many are unaware today that Jesus is soon to come. Even some of those who know He is coming are unprepared for Him.

Our Final Exam

Before an exam it is a good idea to know pretty well what the teacher has been emphasizing. Students cramming for their finals have an advantage if they have some idea of the kind of questions the teacher is going to ask. As we think of that day when we shall meet our Master, it's a good idea to know what He'll expect of us. We need to begin now to cram for our finals. We have been given this insight into the one great question we'll be asked. "'When the Son of man shall come in His glory, and all the holy angels with Him, then shall He sit upon the throne of His glory: and before Him shall be gathered all nations: and He shall separate them from one another.' Thus Christ on the Mount of Olives pictured to His disciples the scene of the great judgment day. And He represented its decision as *turning upon one point*. When the nations are gathered before Him, there will be but two classes, and their eternal destiny will be determined by what they have done or have neglected to do for Him in the person of the poor and the suffering.

"In that day Christ does not present before men the great work He has done for them in giving His life for their redemption. He presents the faithful work they have done for Him. To those whom He sets upon His right hand He will say, 'Come, ye blessed of My Father, inherit the kingdom prepared for you from the foundation of the world: for I was an hungered, and ye gave Me meat: I was thirsty, and ye gave Me drink: I was a stranger, and ye took Me in: naked, and ye clothed Me: I was sick, and ye visited Me: I was in prison, and ye came unto Me.' But those whom Christ commends know not that they have been ministering unto Him. To their perplexed inquiries He answers, 'Inasmuch as ye have done it unto one of the least of these My brethren, ye have done it unto Me'" (*The Desire of Ages*, p. 637, italics supplied).

Matthew 25:34-36 (cited in the quotation above) describes how Jesus' love is to be seen in us. Additional emphasis is given in these words: "There is nothing that Christ desires so much as agents who will represent to the world His Spirit and character. There is nothing that the world needs so much as the manifestation through humanity of the Saviour's love. All heaven is waiting for channels through which can be poured the holy oil to be a joy and blessing to human hearts" (*Christ's Object Lessons*, p. 419).

One day soon, you and I will meet the Master. It will not be a day of our own choosing. When we meet Him we will be aware of His great, overwhelming love for us, for we shall see with our own eyes the scars on His brow and the nailprints in His hands.

There will be *only one question* asked on that day—but it will reveal the extent, it will reveal the depths, of our love for Him. We cannot wait until that moment to formulate the answer. We are doing that today in the way we relate to those about us and in our use of the time he has given us to employ in His service.

Chapter 12
"He Humbled Himself"

Matthew 26 moves from the heights of adoration and self-denial to the depths of treachery and disciple-denial. Here we find Jesus, who "thought it not robbery to be equal with God" (Philippians 2:6), humbling Himself and becoming "obedient unto death, even the death of the cross" (Philippians 2:8) as He accepted the cup in our behalf in Gethsemane.

But first there was that act of adoration that sustained Him in the hour of suffering and temptation. Shame, fear and embarrassment did not prevent Mary, the sister of Lazarus and Martha, who also was known as Mary Magdalene, from performing that simple act of love which has never been forgotten. Disregarding the jealous comments of those who cared less for Jesus than she did, Mary poured out her gift of love for her Redeemer at Simon's feast that took place on the first Saturday night of what we call Passion Week.

We are living in the time when Jesus is to return. If we are to ever open our hearts of love and pour out our gifts of love upon His feet—*now is the time*. Soon it will be too late; our gifts will have no meaning.

On the island of Okinawa we saw the hills around Naha covered with elaborate tombs. The Okinawan people, who did not have much in the way of worldly goods when we were there, lavish thousands of dollars on the tombs of their dead. We could not help but think how much more worthwhile it would be to give their gifts of love while their loved ones were still alive and could appreciate them.

Soon the time will be past when we can honor Jesus with our substance. Soon material things will have no meaning. Now is the time to demonstrate our love and affection for Him in every way He makes it possible for us to do so.

Christ's Response to Treachery

It probably is not coincidental that Matthew juxtaposes Mary's unstinting gift of love with Judas's despicable deed of treachery. Both are recognized today as the epitome in their category of behavior. The pouring out of the priceless ointment and loving tears on the feet of Jesus contrasts so startlingly with betraying Him for thirty pieces of silver.

Because they were convinced that Jesus was about to establish an earthly kingdom, the disciples had been jockeying for the most prominent positions in that kingdom. We might well wonder how it was that some of them who had lived and worked with Jesus for nearly three years had listened to words from heaven and seen them demonstrated in His life, yet had not grasped the basic concepts He taught and lived. How could they be so unprepared to carry on the work He expected them to do when He left? How could they be so callous as to be struggling for position in His kingdom on the night they saw their kingdom hopes dashed as He was taken from them in Gethsemane?

Where were they carrying on this inappropriately strange debate? At the table where Jesus was to eat the Last Supper with them. Instead of scolding them, however, Jesus startled them with a remarkable demonstration of unselfish love. As the Lord of the universe knelt to wash their travel-dusty feet, their pride and selfishness were rebuked. His dramatic act not only washed their feet, but also washed away their pride, except for that of the betrayer. "Even after he [Judas] had twice pledged himself to betray the Saviour, there was opportunity for repentance. At the Passover supper Jesus proved His divinity by revealing the traitor's purpose. He tenderly included Judas in the ministry to the disciples. But the last appeal of love was unheeded. Then the case of Judas was decided, and the feet that Jesus had washed went forth to the betrayer's work" (*The Desire of Ages*, p. 720).

Matthew begins his account of the Last Supper with Jesus' statement that one of those at the table was to betray Him (see Matthew 26:21). Although the disciples did not catch on fully that the traitor was Judas, the betrayer realized that Jesus knew what he had done. In not publicly denouncing him, Jesus made a final attempt to reconcile Judas to Him. "But when he left the presence of his Lord and his fellow disciples, the final decision had been made. He had passed the boundary line" (*The Desire of Ages*, pp. 654, 655).

For some reason Matthew chose not to give us the kind of detailed information that John did about what went on in the upper room. Chapter 13 of the Gospel of John closes with the first part of the Lord's upper room discourse. The first twelve chapters of John emphasize the witness to the fact that Jesus was the expected Messiah (the Christ). Beginning with John 13, the emphasis shifts to the glorification of the Messiah. The first part of chapter 13 demonstrates how Jesus was glorified in humility. He *stooped* to *great heights* when He washed His disciples' feet. But He was to stoop even higher in the events that were soon to follow.

How was Jesus to achieve His greatest glory? Judas's hasty exit was the sign that the betrayal was only a few hours away and that Jesus soon would be crucified. God and Christ would be glorified in the events that made salvation possible to all who accept Jesus' death as the means of being saved.

The New Commandment

We are dependent also on John's account for the story of how Christ gave the new commandment to His disciples that last night they spent together in the upper room. The selfless love that led Jesus to give His life for us demonstrates the kind of love God makes possible for those who accept Christ's salvation. Because it now has been demonstrated, a new commandment can be added to the basic principles of God's law—

love for God and love for our fellow human beings. The new commandment is outlined in John 13:34. Actually, the commandment to love one another was not new (see Leviticus 19:18). What, then, was new about the "new commandment"? Jesus added the thought that we should love "as I have loved you." Never before Jesus came had such a demonstration of God's love been given on earth.

Why must Christ's followers love as He loved? In order for others to see what Christ can do in and for those who submit themselves to Him and as a demonstration of the great love of God to the people of the world.

During those solemn hours in the secluded room in Jerusalem, Jesus had been preparing His disciples for what He termed the hour of His glorification. That glorification was to begin with the ultimate humiliation of betrayal, illegal trial, and crucifixion. But each shameful act in reality glorified the Son of God, who was willing to bear what we deserve that we might share what He deserves.

Gethsemane

So much could be said about the significance of Gethsemane. It was there that Jesus made the conscious decision to accept the cross. There in a garden named for an olive press, the last ounce of the agony and suffering for sin was pressed from the great heart of the Son of God.

The chapter entitled "Gethsemane" in *The Desire of Ages* gives amazing insights into Christ's temptation and struggle in that garden.

1. A marked change took place in Jesus' physical appearance as He approached the garden. He groaned aloud under the pressure of His terrible burden (pp. 685, 686).

2. Jesus fell prostrate upon the ground in agonizing prayer (pp. 686, 690). This contrasts markedly with the familiar paintings that show Him kneeling sedately at a rock.

3. "The humanity of the Son of God trembled in that trying hour" (p. 690).

4. After He had made the decision to accept the cup of suf-

fering for us, Jesus fell dying to the ground. An angel was sent to strengthen Him (p. 693).

Added to His trouble and sorrow was His followers' sleepy indifference to what He was going through. Then came the worst blow of all, the terrible betrayal by one He had loved and labored for.

That the Garden of Gethsemane was one of Jesus' favorite prayer retreats when he was in the Jerusalem area is indicated by John 18:2. This most likely explains why Judas was so sure that he could lead those who wished to capture Jesus without creating a public stir to the place where Jesus was most likely to be

The Trials and Peter's Denial

The agony and suffering did not end even with the betrayal. Much more was to follow. First there was the mockery and torture of the illegal trials. These trials can be outlined as follows:

1. *The Religious Trials*:
    a. The first hearing before Annas—John 18:13-18.
    b. Hearing before Caiaphas—John 18:19-27.
    c. Night trial before the Sanhedrin—Matthew 26:57-75.
    d. Day trial before the Sanhedrin—Luke 22:66-71.
2. *The Political Trials*:
    a. First trial before Pilate—John 18:28-40.
    b. Hearing before Herod—Luke 23:6-12.
    c. Second trial before Pilate—John 19:1-16.

It is difficult for us to appreciate fully what Jesus went through during these trials. We do not have the struggle He had with knowing that he could stop it all by the use of divine power. "Christ suffered keenly under abuse and insult. At the hands of the beings whom He had created, and for whom He was making an infinite sacrifice, He received every indignity. And He suffered in proportion to the perfection of His holiness and His hatred of sin. His trial by men who acted as fiends was to Him a perpetual sacrifice. To be surrounded by human beings under the control of Satan was revolting to Him. And

He knew that in a moment, by the flashing forth of His divine power, he could lay His cruel tormentors in the dust. This made the trial harder to bear" (*The Desire of Ages*, p. 700).

But an even keener anguish was involved in Jesus' "humbling," something even worse than being spat upon. Peter and John followed the mob that left Gethsemane and gained admission to the court of Caiaphas's judgment hall. Peter joined a company about the fire in the court, hoping that no one would recognize him as one of Jesus' disciples. His heart was wrung with sorrow as He saw the indignities heaped on his Master, but he tried to hide his true feelings under a cloak of indifference. There was no way, however, that he could cover up his feelings. Twice those about him noticed the look of dejection that marked his face and charged him with being a follower of Jesus. He replied with an oath that he was not. About an hour later, a kinsman of Malchus, whose ear he had cut off, asked him, "Didn't I see you in the garden with him?" Peter, flying into a rage, denied his link with Jesus. He cursed and swore in order to deceive those who were suspicious about his connection with Christ.

Just then Peter heard a rooster crow. That brought to his mind Jesus' prediction that he would deny his Master three times before the cock crowed. In spite of His agony and suffering, Jesus was aware of Peter's desperation. He turned and looked at Peter. "Peter's eyes were drawn to his Master. In that gentle countenance he read deep pity and sorrow, but there was no anger there.

"The sight of that pale, suffering face, those quivering lips, that look of compassion and forgiveness, pierced his heart like an arrow. . . . Peter had just declared that he knew not Jesus, but he now realized with bitter grief how well his Lord knew him, and how accurately He had read his heart, the falseness of which was unknown even to himself.

" . . . He reflected with horror upon his own ingratitude, his falsehood, his perjury. Once more he looked at his Master, and saw a sacrilegious hand raised to smite Him in the face. Unable longer to endure the scene, he rushed, heartbroken, from the hall" (*The Desire of Ages*, p. 713).

"Let This Mind Be in You"

There was still more to take place in Christ's humbling of Himself "unto death, even the death of the cross" (Philippians 2:8). But Paul records the fact of Christ's humbling in order to challenge us, "Let this mind be in you" (Philippians 2:5). What kind of mind? That "which was also in Christ Jesus," he answers. The word used for Christ's humbling of Himself in this passage connotes "emptying." He gave all He had for us, not just on the cross, but in His acceptance of the terrible torture, betrayal, and denial.

A Scottish preacher, Dr. Durham, was on his way to preach at the church he pastored when he was joined by the popular young minister of a nearby church. The younger preacher had caused quite a sensation with his dynamic sermons and had drawn away several members from Dr. Durham's church. Apologetically, the young minister said, "They are greatly to blame who leave you and come to me."

"Not so, Brother," Dr. Durham replied, "for a minister can receive no such honor and success in his ministry except it be given him from heaven. I rejoice that Christ is preached, and that His kingdom and interests are gaining ground, even though my estimation in people's hearts should decrease. I am content to be anything or nothing so that Christ may be all in all." That's what it means to humble or empty ourselves and have the mind of Christ. He is to be our all in all.

When someone asked Francis of Assisi why he was so influential and seemed to have so much power to touch people's hearts and lives, he replied, "Well, I've been thinking about that myself lately, and this is why: The Lord looked down from heaven upon the earth and said, 'Where can I find the weakest, the littlest, the meanest man on the face of the earth?' Then He saw me and said, 'I've found him! Now I'll work through him. He won't be proud of it. He'll see that I am only using him because of his littleness and insignificance.'"

When we are willing to humble ourselves, to empty ourselves in order to become vessels fully yielded to hold the mercies of God, the Lord will be able to use us. He will fill us full of blessings to bestow on those about us.

Chapter 13
Undercomers Anonymous

"For scarcely for a righteous man will one die; yet perhaps for a good man someone would even dare to die. But God demonstrates His own love toward us, in that while we were still sinners, Christ died for us" (Romans 5:7, 8, NKJV).

The terrible ordeal Jesus underwent during the cruel trials was followed by the even greater ordeal of the cross. Crucifixion was a terrible way to die. Only the worst criminals were put to death that way. Strange as it may seem, the cross, the emblem of the most shameful death possible in the Roman world, has become the glorious emblem of the love of God. When Jesus died on the cross, He decisively defeated sin and death, making eternal life possible for all who choose to take up His cross and follow Him.

Seven Words from the Cross

Many sermons and week of prayer series have been based on Christ's words from the cross. I have arranged them in their most likely sequence:

1. **"Father, forgive them; for they know not what they do" (Luke 23:34).** Actually these words were prayed by Jesus while He was being nailed to the cross. "No curses were called down upon the soldiers who were handling Him so roughly. No vengeance was invoked upon the priests and rulers, who

were gloating over the accomplishment of their purpose. Christ pitied them in their ignorance and guilt. He breathed only a plea for their forgiveness,—'for they know not what they do' " (*The Desire of Ages*, p. 744).

2. **"Verily I say unto thee, To day shalt thou be with me in paradise" (Luke 23:43). (Concordant Version reads: "Verily to you I am saying today, with Me you shall be in the paradise.")** Here again, in spite of His great agony and suffering, Jesus was taking interest in and showing compassion for someone other than Himself.

3. **"Woman behold thy son! . . . Behold thy mother" (John 19:26, 27).** By identifying with her outlawed son at the cross, Mary was cutting herself off from her community and family who did not accept Jesus. Even while undergoing the terrible trauma of crucifixion, Jesus was aware of her great need. Realizing that He would no longer be able to provide for her, He made testamentary provision to place His mother under John's protection and in his home.

4. **"My God, my God, why hast thou forsaken me?" (Matthew 27:46).** At this point Jesus was dying the second death for us. Because the terrible weight of our guilt rested on Him, the Lord was experiencing what the sinner will feel who is eternally lost. It broke His heart (see *The Desire of Ages*, p. 753).

5. **"I thirst" (John 19:28).** At about the ninth hour (3 P.M.) the darkness that had surrounded Christ when He was suffering for our guilt was lifted. "He revived to a sense of physical suffering, and said, 'I thirst' " (*The Desire of Ages*, p. 754). He was offered vinegar to drink from a sponge tied to a reed.

6. **"It is finished" (John 19:30).** These words and the next set seem to have been uttered at the same time. At this moment the evening sacrifice was being offered in the temple. A great earthquake took place. The unseen hand of God rent the inner veil. The knife with which the priest was about to slay the evening sacrifice dropped from his nerveless hand and the lamb escaped (see *The Desire of Ages*, p. 757). At that very moment the Lamb of God died with the words that follow on His lips.

7. **"Father, into thy hands I commend my spirit" (Luke 23:46).** "The battle had been won. His right hand and His holy arm had gotten Him the victory. As a conqueror He planted His banner on the eternal heights. Was there not joy among the angels? All heaven triumphed in the Saviour's victory. Satan was defeated, and knew that his kingdom was lost" (*The Desire of Ages*, p. 758).

The Resurrection of the King

Paul testified: "For I delivered to you first of all that which I also received: that Christ died for our sins according to the Scriptures, and that He was buried, and that He rose again the third day according to the Scriptures" (1 Corinthians 15:3, 4, NKJV).

"The night of the first day of the week had worn slowly away. The darkest hour, just before daybreak, had come. Christ was still a prisoner in His narrow tomb. The great stone was in its place; the Roman seal was unbroken; the Roman guards were keeping their watch" (*The Desire of Ages*, pp. 779).

Then came one of the greatest events ever witnessed by human beings—the resurrection of Christ (see the magnificent description in *The Desire of Ages*, pp. 779-781). Because of what happened the day Jesus arose from Joseph's new tomb, a journey to the grave today is but a round trip for those who fall asleep in Jesus. The assurance of our eternal life rests on the resurrection of Christ. The most convincing evidence of His resurrection is the testimony of the believer to the presence and power of the risen Christ in his or her life.

Witnesses to the Resurrection

"Christ's first work on earth after His resurrection was to convince His disciples of His undiminished love and tender regard for them. To give them proof that He was their living Saviour, that he had broken the fetters of the tomb, and could no longer be held by the enemy death; to reveal that He had the same heart of love as when He was with them as their beloved Teacher, He appeared to them again and again. He would draw the bonds of love still closer around them" (*The Desire of Ages*, p. 793).

None of the Gospel writers list all of the ten appearances of Christ after the resurrection. In order to get a complete picture, we must put their records together:

1. John 20:11-18—Appearance to Mary at the tomb.

2. Matthew 28:8-10—Appearance to Mary Magdalene and the "other" Mary on their way to report the empty tomb to the disciples.

3. Luke 24:34; 1 Corinthians 15:5—Appearance to Peter before appearing to the rest of the disciples.

4. Luke 24:13-35—Appearance to two disciples on the way to Emmaus.

5. John 20:19-23—Appearance to ten disciples in the upper room on Sunday evening. Thomas was absent.

6. John 20:26-29—Appearance to the disciples, including Thomas, in the upper room one week later.

7. John 21:1-14—Appearance to seven disciples some time later when they were fishing in the Sea of Galilee.

8. Matthew 28:16-20; 1 Corinthians 15:6—Appearance to the disciples and 500 others on a mountain in Galilee.

9. 1 Corinthians 15:7—"After that, he was seen of James."

10. Luke 24:50, 51; Acts 1:2-9—Appearance to the disciples as He walked with them from Jerusalem to Bethany, then ascended to heaven.

Thus there were innumerable witnesses to the victory of Jesus over sin, death, and the grave. The glorious fact is that He won that victory for us. Satan is a defeated foe. Even though we still must struggle personally with sin and temptation, our victory is assured if we take full advantage of what Jesus did for us on Calvary.

His Victory Is Ours

Jesus did not come to demonstrate in His life on earth what a God can do, but to show what fallen people like us can become through the grace and power of God. The truly good news of the gospel is that fallen, sinful beings *can* overcome sin. By God's grace, we can be more than conquerors (see Romans 8:37). By the infilling and continual presence of the Holy Spirit, from the time He was born, Christ demonstrated the ability of those who are born again to overcome evil. We are given this insight into how this works:

"It is the Spirit that makes effectual what has been wrought out by the world's Redeemer. It is by the Spirit that the heart is made pure. Through the Spirit the believer becomes a partaker of the divine nature. Christ has given His Spirit as a divine power to overcome all hereditary and cultivated tendencies to evil, and to impress His own character upon His church" (*The Desire of Ages*, p. 671).

I have heard some mutter, "That's impossible!" when faced with the challenge of overcoming all sin. They're right. It is impossible—for us to accomplish on our own without Christ. But Paul found that "I can do all things through Christ which strengtheneth me" (Philippians 4:13).

It was impossible for Barbara Sechrist, with her bad back, to lift a 500-pound tombstone that was crushing little Heather Isgate to death. But she did it. Mrs. Sechrist attributes the abnormal strength she exhibited in freeing Heather to God giving her the strength to do it. Mrs. Sechrist and her class were walking through a cemetery on a Sunday School excursion when Heather walked over to a tombstone and put her arms around it. The heavy stone toppled over, pinning her down.

When Mrs. Sechrist tried to lift the stone she found that she could not budge it. She prayed to God to help her, then tried again. This time she was able to lift it. Heather suffered a cracked rib and broken ankle, but her life had been saved by what should have been an impossible feat.

We serve a God who makes all things possible, even overcoming sin. If He were not able to do so, the seven promises to the overcomer in Revelation 2 and 3 would be mere taunts. Instead, they are precious promises. What God challenges us to do, He makes possible.

What strategies have you found to be most effective in dealing with temptation? It should be obvious to each of us by now that we cannot overcome on our own. Our adversary is too strong for us. But he is a defeated foe. Jesus has gained the victory for us if we will let Him win the battle for us. Some ways we cooperate are by:

1. Avoiding places and situations that we know are likely to tempt us.

2. Overcoming evil habits by replacing them with good habits.

3. Hiding God's word in our memory to help us recognize His will in every situation.

4. Developing such a great love for Christ that we would rather die than disappoint Him.

5. Being constantly in an attitude of prayer and communion with God.

6. Attending faithfully Sabbath School, church services, and prayer meetings.

7. Organizing prayer and study groups with five or six church members who live in our area.

8. Not neglecting Bible study. Particularly spending some time each day contemplating the life of Jesus.

When Satan comes to dispute, call on the Lord to rebuke him. When he is tempting and bargaining with you, appeal to God's holy Word, "It is written." And when he is using another individual to attack you, trust in Christ to rebuke that person instead of trying to do it yourself.

If you are not yet an *over*comer, then you must be the opposite, an *under*comer. If you are, I challenge you to become a charter member in a club I'm forming called Undercomers Anonymous. All you have to do to belong is believe that Jesus' victory can be yours and be willing to let God help you overcome all sin in your life. You can cooperate with Him in this work of grace by following the eight steps just listed.

In his book entitled *Lyrics*, Oscar Hammerstein II illustrates the fact that the building of our characters has to be a thorough work. There cannot be any hidden or neglected weaknesses. He reports seeing a picture of the top of the

Statue of Liberty's head taken from a helicopter. He was amazed to notice the painstaking detail that marked the sculptor's work on that part of the statue only the uncritical eyes of sea gulls would ever be expected to see. The sculptor was enough of an artist to finish off this part of the statue with as much careful detail as that devoted to its more visible parts.

Someday soon every inch of the characters that we have allowed God to build in us will be subjected to minute scrutiny by the Judge of the universe. Because He has promised us unlimited aid in finishing the job of character building, we will have no excuse for neglecting any, what may seem unimportant, detail. If we let Him, He will enable us to overcome every cultivated and inherited tendency to evil. That's how great and all-encompassing Christ's victory was. It reaches down to every one of us today, guaranteeing us victory, too—victory over Satan, self, sin, and death.

Sitting at his custom booth in Capernaum, Levi Matthew looked into the loving, appealing eyes of One he recognized as wanting to become his Saviour. When Jesus invited Matthew to give up all and follow Him, the greedy publican did not stop to count and record the day's receipts lying there on the table before him. He recognized in Christ's glance the promise of greater, eternal riches and immediately left his business, consecrating all that he had and was to the Lord for the rest of his life. Can we do any less? As the Master bids us take up His cross and follow Him, we see in His loving glance the promise of what we can become through the power of His grace. As we reach out to accept His cross we discover what He hands us is, instead, His crown of victory.